OXFORD BIBLE SERIES

General Editors
P. R. Ackroyd and G. N. Stanton

Wisdom and Law in the Old Testament

The Ordering of Life in Israel and Early Judaism

JOSEPH BLENKINSOPP

OXFORD UNIVERSITY PRESS
1983

Oxford University Press, Walton Street, Oxford OX2 6DP

London Glasgow New York Toronto
Delhi Bombay Calcutta Madras Karachi
Kuala Lumpur Singapore Hong Kong Tokyo
Nairobi Dar es Salaam Cape Town
Melbourne Auckland
and associates in
Beirut Berlin Ibadan Mexico City Nicosia

Oxford is a trade mark of Oxford University Press

Published in the United States by
Oxford University Press, New York

British Library Cataloguing in Publication Data
Blenkinsopp, Joseph
Wisdom and law in the Old Testament.
– (Oxford Bible series)
1. Bible. O.T. – Commentaries
I. Title
221.7   BS1151.2
ISBN 0-19-213253-9

Library of Congress Cataloging in Publication Data
Blenkinsopp, Joseph, 1927–
Wisdom and law in the Old Testament.
(The Oxford Bible series)
Bibliography: p.
Includes index.
1. Wisdom literature.   2. Law – Biblical teaching.
3. Jewish law.   4. Bible. O.T. – Criticism, inter-
pretation, etc.   I. Title.   II. Series.
BS1455.B53 1983   221.6   82-24658
ISBN 0-19-213253-9 (pbk.)

Typeset by Hope Services, Abingdon, Oxon
Printed in the United States of America

GENERAL EDITORS' PREFACE

There are many commentaries on individual books of the Bible, but the reader who wishes to take a broader view has less choice. This series is intended to meet this need. Its structure is thematic, with each volume embracing a number of biblical books. It is designed for use with any of the familiar translations of the Bible; quotations are normally from RSV, but the authors of the individual volumes also use other translations or make their own where this helps to bring out the particular meaning of a passage.

To provide general orientation, there are two volumes of a more introductory character: one will consider the Old Testament in its cultural and historical context, the other the New Testament, discussing the origins of Christianity. Four volumes deal with different kinds of material in the Old Testament: narrative, prophecy, poetry/psalmody, wisdom and law. Three volumes handle different aspects of the New Testament: the Gospels, Paul and Pauline Christianity, the varieties of New Testament thought. One volume looks at the nature of biblical interpretation, covering both Testaments.

The authors of the individual volumes write for a general readership. Technical terms and Hebrew or Greek words are explained; the latter are used only when essential to the understanding of the text. The general introductory volumes are designed to stand on their own, providing a framework, but also to serve to raise some of the questions which the remaining volumes examine in closer detail. All the volumes other than the two general ones include a discussion of selected biblical passages in greater depth, thus providing examples of the ways in which the interpretation of the text makes possible deeper understanding of the wider issues, both historical and theological, with which the Bible is concerned. Select bibliographies in each volume point the way to further discussion of the many issues which remain open to fuller exploration.

67628

P. R. A.
G. N. S.

NOTE

CONTENTS

KEY PASSAGES DISCUSSED

1

Sages, Scribes, and Counsellors

The Writings

In the Hebrew Bible the books over and above Pentateuch and Prophets are listed simply as Writings (*ketubim* in Hebrew). The resulting tripartite distinction is first clearly attested in the Prologue to Ben Sira (Ecclesiasticus), written about 130 BC, which refers to 'the law, the prophets, and the other books of our fathers'. Ben Sira's own account of the scribal profession, to which he himself belonged, lists Torah, the wisdom of the ancients, and prophecy as the principal objects of study (39: 1). Despite the different order, which corresponds to that of the Greek Bible, this too may indicate a mature stage in the emergence of a tripartite canon. It would also suggest that the Writings were meant to provide a cross-section of the accumulated wisdom of the past as a guide for living in the present; or, as Josephus would put it nearly three centuries later, 'precepts for the conduct of human life' (*Against Apion* 1: 40).

Unlike the first two sections of the canon, however, the Writings do not exhibit any obvious principle of unity. From the literary point of view, they include historiography (1 and 2 Chronicles, Ezra, Nehemiah), edifying fiction (Esther, Daniel 1-6, Ruth), lyrics (Song of Songs), hymns (Psalms, Lamentations), dialogue (Job), monologue (Ecclesiastes), proverbs with other didactic genres (Proverbs) and apocalyptic (Daniel 7-12). The list will be even longer if we include books which came to be part of the Greek Bible or Septuagint. The common practice of referring to this heterogeneous collection as 'wisdom writings' would seem, then, to call for an explanation. Very few of these compositions (Proverbs, Ecclesiastes, perhaps Job) can be called sapiential in the sense of imparting instruction or addressing themselves to broad issues of a philosophical or theological nature. At the purely literary level, therefore, the designation is clearly inadequate. The situation may, however, look rather different if we take into account the existence of an authoritative sapiential tradition within which a wide variety of literary forms could be located. A good example would be the Song of Songs.

On the face of it, this composition would appear to be a series of erotic poems in the courtly style. The precise determination of genre is a matter of dispute. Some commentators, impressed by the dialogue between courtesan and shepherd, have thought of it as a drama, perhaps with undertones of the cultic drama associated with a fertility myth. For our present purpose it is not important to decide this issue. What is important is that it is attributed to Solomon even though the fiction is not evenly maintained throughout the work. By the time of writing, the tradition about Solomon as supreme example of the sage was firmly established. An important aspect, illustrated by the well-known story of the two women claiming the same child (1 Kgs. 3: 16-28), had to do with the administration of justice, the most important function of monarchy. The visit of the queen of Sheba to Solomon's court, during which he successfully answered the hard questions she put to him (1 Kgs. 10: 1-10), demonstrated that his wisdom was equal to that of the Arabs, proverbial for sagacity. The historian sums it up as follows:

> God gave Solomon wisdom and understanding beyond measure, and largeness of mind like the sand on the seashore, so that Solomon's wisdom surpassed the wisdom of all the people of the east . . . and his fame was in the nations round about. He also uttered three thousand proverbs; and his songs were a thousand and five. He spoke of trees, from the cedar that is in Lebanon to the hyssop that grows out of the wall; he spoke also of beasts, and of birds, and of reptiles, and of fish. And men came from all peoples to hear the wisdom of Solomon, and from all the kings of the earth, who had heard of his wisdom. [1 Kgs. 4: 29-34]

The title 'the Song of Songs which is Solomon's' implies the writer's intent to present it as the most excellent of the thousand and five composed by Solomon. And since Solomon's wisdom (which included literary ability) came to him as a divine gift bestowed in a vision (1 Kgs. 3: 4-14), there is the further implication of divine inspiration. To attribute a book to Solomon, therefore, was a way of bringing it within the sapiential tradition and bestowing on it a special authority. Thus, the two longer collections in Proverbs are presented as a selection of the three thousand which Solomon uttered (Prov. 10: 1; 25: 1) and the book itself was published under his name (1: 1). Despite some disconcerting views which it expresses, Ecclesiastes (Qoheleth) found its way into the canon under the same imprimatur. The tradition was carried on in the Wisdom of Solomon, the Odes of Solomon and, eventually, in the esoteric writings of Jewish (and other) cabbalists and mystics into the Middle Ages and beyond.

We may therefore conclude that the Song of Songs, though obviously not a didactic composition, was seen to contain a message which the sages wished to recommend with all the authority of an age-old tradition. Without going into the interpretation of the book, in dispute since late antiquity, we may simply note how it gives pride of place to the mystery and the power of love between woman and man. The point is made in the one generalizing statement in the book, towards the end, which is probably editorial:

> Many waters cannot quench love,
>   neither can floods drown it.
> If a man offered for love
>   all the wealth of his house,
>   it would be utterly scorned.   (8: 7)

Despite the many proverbs which exhibit an ungenerous and petulant attitude to women, the theme is by no means foreign to the tradition in which the writer or editor stood. There is the numerical proverb (Prov. 30: 18-19, to be discussed in the next chapter) about the way of a man with a maid and the question addressed to the young man tempted to adultery:

> Can a man carry fire in his bosom
>   and his clothes not be burned?   (Prov. 6: 27)

Indeed, at one point we find the same kind of imagery as in the Song of Songs:

> Drink water from your own cistern,
>   flowing water from your own well.
> Should your springs be scattered abroad,
>   streams of water in the streets? . . .
> Let your fountain be blessed,
>   and rejoice in the wife of your youth,
>   a lovely hind, a graceful doe.
> Let her affection fill you at all times with delight,
>   be infatuated always with her love. (Prov. 5: 15-19)

We do not have to exclude this intention in order to affirm that the sexual imagery can also be referred to the bond between God and Israel as his spouse. Given the development of this theme in the eighth-century prophet Hosea, and the powerful influence which it continued to exert, the reference was surely inevitable. In this respect it may be significant that Hosea is the only prophetic book which ends with a colophon couched in the language of the sages:

> Whoever is wise, let him understand these things;
> Whoever is discerning, let him know them. (14: 9)

According to traditional accounts, the canon of the Hebrew Scriptures was fixed by Ezra and the men of the Great Assembly, a legislative body which included the last of the prophets and other worthies, one hundred and twenty in all. Whatever doubts remained about individual books, including the Song of Songs, were settled at a synod held (*c.* AD 100) at Jamnia (Yavneh), the intellectual centre of Judaism after the disastrous war with Rome. While this reconstruction of the formation of the canon has rightly been abandoned by critical scholarship, it may serve to indicate the important role played in this process by the scribes, represented by Ezra, and their successors, the leaders of the early rabbinic academies. Later in this chapter we shall see how the influence and prestige of the scribal schools steadily increased throughout the period of the Second Temple. There are also indications, which will be noted at the appropriate point, that the sages took over the prophetic claim to mediate revelation. It was by virtue of such a claim that the canon came to be extended to cover a miscellaneous body of writings over and above the Law and the Prophets.

The many faces of wisdom

If we begin by surveying the vocabulary denoting wisdom in the Hebrew Bible, we see that very often it stands for the possession of a particular skill, e.g., that of the goldsmith (Jer. 10: 9), stonemason (1 Chr. 22: 15) or ship-builder (Ezek. 27: 8-9). Bezalel and his colleagues who were commissioned to make the tent and the ark were 'wise' in the sense that they were endowed with the necessary technical and artistic skill (Ex. 31: 1-11; 35: 30 – 36: 1). A special case would be that of the magician's art (e.g. Isa. 3: 3) corresponding to the kind of competence expected of sages in ancient Egypt, at least as the Israelites viewed them (Gen. 41: 8; Ex. 7: 11). As for the 'wise women' mentioned here and there in the record (2 Sam. 14: 2; 20: 16), the emphasis seems to be more on persuasive speech than the magical arts. Following well-established precedent, however, wisdom *par excellence* belonged to the ruler. The wise woman from Tekoa, who succeeded in persuading David to recall his son from exile, seems to have been well acquainted with this convention in ascribing to him 'wisdom like the angel of God to know all things that are on the earth' (2 Sam. 14: 20). And in the person of his son Solomon, as we have seen, royal wisdom reached its fullest expression.

The passage to monarchy necessitated royal counsellors trained in the international conventions of diplomacy and schooled in an intellectual tradition which had little in common with the piety and cult of the tribal past. The inevitable tensions between this new wisdom of international stamp and indigenous resources (e.g. appeal to an oracle or a seer for guidance) come to a head in the court history covering the last years of David's reign (2 Sam. 11-20; 1 Kgs. 1-2). There is a certain structural unity to the narrative which begins with Solomon's birth and ends with his accession. A first episode deals with Amnon the crown prince (2 Sam. 13). Wishing to possess himself of his beautiful half-sister Tamar, he sought advice of David's nephew Jonadab described as 'a very wise man' (13: 3). Jonadab's wisdom turned out to be the kind of guile which enabled him to propose a plan whereby Amnon could have his will of Tamar. The plan worked, but it led to the death of Amnon, assassinated by

Absalom as he lay in a drunken stupor. In due course Absalom, exiled from the court as a result of avenging his sister's honour, was brought back by the wiles of a 'wise woman' hired by the army commander Joab (2 Sam. 14). This too had fateful consequences, leading to Absalom's rebellion and, eventually, his death in battle.

The paradox of wisdom which leads to disaster and death is exemplified most vividly in the person of Ahithophel, David's counsellor, who joined Absalom's conspiracy and rebellion. His prestige was such that 'the counsel which Ahithophel gave was as if one consulted the oracle of God' (16: 23). David prayed to Yahweh to turn that counsel into foolishness (15: 31), and the subsequent course of the narrative shows how the prayer was answered. Ahithophel's advice, to attack David at once before he had time to consolidate his position, was correct, but it was countered by that of Hushai, another sage left behind by David to deceive the unsuspecting Absalom. At this point the writer makes one of his infrequent intrusions into the story with the comment that

> Yahweh had ordained to defeat the good counsel of Ahithophel, so that Yahweh might bring evil upon Absalom.   (17: 14)

The episode then comes to an end with Ahithophel's suicide (17: 23).

The ambiguities of wisdom are illustrated in a remarkably similar way in the narrative of the Man in the Garden of Eden which is part of the primeval history (Gen. 2: 4 − 3: 24). While the mythic basis of the story can be shown to derive from ancient Mesopotamia, a Canaanite version existed and was used by Ezekiel in his lamentation over the king of Tyre (Ezek. 28: 12-19). It would, however, be misleading to describe the story in Genesis simply as a myth. It is, rather, an excellent example of the ability of the sages to make learned use of mythological tradition for their own ends. In other respects, too, the sapiential character of the narrative is apparent; suffice it to note the interest in ancient geography (the four rivers, 2: 10-14) and the Man's naming of the animals (2: 19-20), an anticipation of Solomon's onomastic wisdom, that is, his skill in naming, and therefore ordering, things (1 Kgs. 4: 33). As in Ezekiel's poem, the Man who is to lose his innocence for ever starts out 'full of wisdom, perfect in beauty'.

With the entry of the serpent into the story, we have another example of a wise agent following whose advice leads to ruinous consequences. The function of the serpent is expressed in a punning use of the Hebrew word *'arum* which can mean 'naked' or 'cunning':

> The man and his wife were both *'arumim* (naked), and were not ashamed; and the serpent was more *'arum* (naked/cunning) than any other wild creature that Yahweh God had made. (2: 25 – 3: 1)

In a sense, of course, snakes are naked or hairless in contrast to most other animals. They are also represented in ancient Near Eastern myth and iconography as both symbolizing the phallus and bringing secret knowledge and wisdom out of the earth where they live. In the story, the snake's strategy is to get the woman, and through her the man, to eat of the tree of knowledge of good and evil. Commentators have ranged far and wide in an attempt to determine the meaning of this phrase and, therefore the symbolic function of the tree. For our present purpose the story itself tells us all we need to know: that the tree was capable of conferring wisdom (3: 6). The implication is that the couple did in fact obtain wisdom, but a wisdom which brought on them the judgment of death.

Both the court history in Samuel and the story in Genesis acknowledge the reality and power of a wisdom which relies exclusively on human resources and autonomous reason. They also reflect the anxious knowledge that to follow it is to risk alienation from the God who called Israel into existence and gave her her destiny. The ensuing tension – apparent, for example, in prophetic polemic against royal counsellors (Isa. 5: 18-23; 29: 14; 30: 1-2) – remained a prominent feature of public life during the monarchy.

The professional sage

The professional dispenser of wisdom in the ancient Near East belonged to a small and privileged élite with a high sense of its own calling. A text from ancient Egypt says of scribes that 'their mortuary service is gone; their tombstones are covered with dirt; and their graves are forgotten. But their names are still pronounced because of their books which they made, since they were good and the memory of him who made them lasts to the limits of eternity'. Another Egyptian classic, from the late third or early second millennium, contrasts a range of other occupations — barber, construction worker, gardener — unfavourably with the scribe and concludes, 'behold, there is no profession free of a boss — except for the scribe: he is the boss'. In the same vein Ben Sira reserves the pursuit of wisdom to the leisured class to which he himself belonged:

> The wisdom of the scribe depends on the opportunity of leisure;
> and he who has little business may become wise. (38: 24)

Compared with prophets and priests, we know very little of this class during the time of the monarchy. While the term *ḥakam* (wise) is used of many individuals, it is very rarely possible to read into it a reference to a distinct category or class. By contrast, there are many allusions to foreign sages. Those of Egypt are skilled in dream interpretation (Gen. 41: 8) and the magical arts (Ex. 7: 11) and serve as counsellors to pharaohs (Isa. 19: 11-12). Much the same can be said of Babylonian sages (Jer. 50: 35; 51: 57; Dan. 2: 12, etc.) and those of other lands noted for their wisdom such as Phoenicia and Edom. Public officials and royal counsellors in Israel thought of themselves as wise, and may have been known as *ḥakamim*, though the claim did not go uncontested (e.g. Isa. 5: 18-23; 29: 14). The nearest we come to a specific class of that name is in the words attributed to those who conspired against Jeremiah: 'Come, let us make plots against Jeremiah, for the law shall not perish from the priest, nor counsel from the wise, nor the word from the prophet'. (18: 18; cf. Ezek. 7: 26 which has 'elders' for 'wise'). Thus, counsel, professional advice, was the province of the sage as instruction in the laws that of the priest. The general impression, then, is that with the passage to monarchy there came into existence a class of royal counsellors or cabinet ministers whose responsibility was to give wise counsel and who were referred to generically as sages (*ḥakamim*).

This conclusion is confirmed by the many allusions throughout the history of the monarchy to a royal official called the scribe (*sopher*). As the name suggests, the basic responsibility of this post was to write; a not unimportant task at a time when writing was a specialist occupation. Nothing much is known of these officials from the earlier period except their names (2 Sam. 8: 16-17; 20: 25; 1 Kgs. 4: 3; 2 Kgs. 12: 10). It appears, however, that they played an important role in matters of state, serving on royal commissions, overseeing the running of the temple, taking part in diplomatic missions and negotiations with foreign powers. The best-known examples are Shebna during the reign of Hezekiah (2 Kgs. 18-19; Is. 22: 15-25) and Shaphan who had an equally distinguished career in the service of Josiah (2 Kgs. 22). The royal scribe occupied a post of broader and more official responsibility than that of counsellors such as Ahithophel and Hushai, while both functions came within the vaguer category of 'the wise'. The milieu of this kind of wisdom, then, was the royal court and the aristocratic circle with which the monarchy surrounded itself.

The historian of the monarchy records that, during the reign of Josiah (640-609 BC), the high priest discovered a law book in the course of carrying out repairs to the temple fabric and that, after authentication by a prophetess, this law was officially promulgated in Jerusalem (2 Kgs. 22: 8 − 23: 3). The identity and origin of this law, and especially the question of its relationship with Deuteronomy, will be dealt with in Chapter 4. What needs to be said now is that such a law requires interpretation and will therefore necessarily bring with it a class of legal specialists. It is hardly coincidental that we hear of such specialists for the first time from Jeremiah who was roughly contemporary with Josiah:

> The priests did not say, 'Where is Yahweh?'
> Those who handle the law did not know me;
> the rulers transgressed against me ...   (Jer. 2: 8)

This category is therefore distinct from the priests who from the earliest times were the custodians of the legal tradition. Elsewhere Jeremiah castigates those who claim to be wise on the grounds of possessing a *written* law and suggests that its meaning had been perverted by the scribes:

> How can you say, 'We are wise,
>   and the law of Yahweh is with us'?
> But, behold, the false pen of the scribes
>   has made it into a lie.
> The wise men shall be put to shame,
>   they shall be dismayed and taken;
> lo, they have rejected the word of Yahweh,
>   and what wisdom is in them?   (8: 8-9)

The implication seems to be that a class of professional legal experts — no doubt identical with the 'handlers of the law' mentioned earlier — was offering authoritative interpretations of the law and that this activity was seen by Jeremiah to pose a threat to his authority as prophet. These scribes were quite distinct from the royal officials whom we have just discussed. There may be connections with the central judiciary required by the Deuteronomic law (Deut. 17: 8-13), but the new and disturbing element for Jeremiah was the claim that the will of Yahweh could be circumscribed by a written law and its authoritative interpretations to the exclusion of the prophetic word.

This saying of Jeremiah gives us our first reference to law scribes as a distinct category. After the restoration of the Judaean community in the Persian period they were to assume increasing importance. According to the Chronicler, our principal source for the period, they belonged for the most part to the clerical ranks. At the great assembly convened by Ezra for the reading of the law book, the necessary commentary and interpretation were supplied by Levites (Neh. 8: 7-8). In his history of the monarchy he also represents levitical scribes as active during the reigns of David (1 Chr. 24: 6) and Josiah (2 Chr. 34: 13), and has Levites touring the country giving instruction in the law (2 Chr. 17: 7-9). Ezra himself is both priest and scribe and his principal concern is the study of the law (Ezra 7: 10 etc.). Later still, the scribe Ben Sira is first and foremost a legal scholar (Ecclus. 32: 14-15; 39: 1) and teaches his discipline in a school (51: 23). Other teachers and sages were active during this long period, including Qoheleth and those whose sayings were brought together by the editor of Proverbs (1: 6; 22: 17; 24: 23; 30: 1; 31: 1). Increasingly, however, the interpretation of and instruction in the law took centre stage and became the vital link with Judaism of the post-biblical period.

Education in Israel

It will be apparent from the previous section that the sages of Israel were primarily teachers. The literature which they produced itself attests to this. Prov. 13: 14, for example, describes the teaching of the wise as a fountain of life, and the epilogue to Ecclesiastes, from a later hand, identifies the author explicitly as a teacher (12: 9). The prologue to Proverbs states quite clearly that the purpose of the collection is

> That men may know wisdom and instruction,
>   understand words of insight,
> receive instruction in wise dealing,
>   righteousness, justice and equity;
> that prudence may be given to the simple,
>   knowledge and discretion to the youth ...   (1: 2-4)

Since, therefore, the 'wisdom literature' of Israel was rooted in the institution of the school, it may be useful to summarize what little is known of education in Israel before going on to examine that literature in detail.

To begin on a rather discouraging note, we have practically no information on the education of the young in the period preceding the establishment of the state. In a participatory society which was primarily agrarian, and in which the basic structures were those of kinship, the kind of educational apparatus with which we are familiar today was neither possible nor necessary. What was needed to equip the child or youth to fulfil his function in society (we are speaking almost exclusively of males) was provided by the extended family in which the elders played a dominant role, not least in inculcating the kind of traditional ethic which held the society together. Even when formulated at a later time, occasional allusions to things which are 'not done in Israel' (e.g. 2 Sam. 13: 12) and injunctions to pass on and explain religious traditions to children (e.g. Ex. 12: 26-7) reflect such a situation.

With gradual assimilation to what remained of Canaanite culture of the Late Bronze Age, the opportunity for a more formal kind of education would have been available to the children of the wealthier and more prominent inhabitants of the cities. A tablet discovered at Shechem in the Central Highlands, dating from the beginning of the fourteenth century, records the complaint of a teacher (who refers to himself as 'father') addressed to a parent delinquent in the payment of the equivalent of school fees. An agricultural calendar inscribed on a small limestone tablet, discovered at Gezer in 1908 and generally dated to the early monarchy, has been widely interpreted as a schoolboy's exercise, though this is quite uncertain. Despite the paucity of hard facts, there can be little doubt that schools existed to teach the different skills necessary for urban living at that time.

In several respects the most important skill of all was writing. Essential for the conduct of diplomacy, it was also increasingly required for the administration of law and estate management. In the Sumerian city-states writing was taught in schools as early as the third millennium BC. The literary remains recovered from such centres (Uruk, Shuruppak, etc.), including proverbs, fables, precepts, and student exercises, necessarily presuppose such institutions. The same situation obtained in Egypt where the scribal profession was held in the highest honour. The thousands of tablets recovered from ancient Ugarit (Ras Shamra) on the Syrian coast, closer to ancient Israel both geographically and culturally, provide indications pointing in the same direction. While therefore we know practically nothing about the management or curriculum of such institutions, there can be little doubt that they existed in Canaan at the time of the Israelite occupation.

The change to monarchy led to the demand for trained personnel to serve the state in a variety of capacities. Of the state officials mentioned in the history one of the most important was the scribe (*sopher*) mentioned earlier in this chapter. The scribe was, of course, trained to write, and there are allusions to such tools of the trade as his pen (Jer. 8: 8), penknife for sharpening quills (Jer. 36: 23) and writing case (Ezek. 9: 2-3). We have already noted, however, that his competence went far beyond writing, including skill in public speaking, negotiation with foreign powers, and financial administration. From the historian's account of the parleying under the gates of Jerusalem during the siege of 701 BC (2 Kgs. 18: 26), it also appears that the scribe could be expected to know the diplomatic language of the period, in this case Aramaic. There are indications that the royal scribe exercised some jurisdiction over the state cult (2 Kgs. 12: 10; 22: 3-10), the temple had its own scribes (Jer. 36: 10-12, 20-1; 37: 15) and so did the army (2 Kgs. 25: 19). A scribe called Baruch attached himself to Jeremiah, wrote his sayings from dictation and read them from a scroll in the temple (Jer. 36). All of this is unintelligible without a fairly well-developed educational institution set up in Jerusalem, very probably on the Egyptian model.

Since the scribal schools existed to prepare the sons of the well-to-do for public service or a life at court, the emphasis was on correct comportment, etiquette, and public speaking. The literary models used for training in writing were most probably translated from Egyptian or at least based on Egyptian school texts. To judge by the extant examples of such texts, the instruction they contained would have emphasized such things as self-control, learning from experience, drawing lessons from the observation of nature. While it would be misleading to speak of it as secular in character, it had little if anything to do with religious traditions and cult. The political pragmatism and rationality of officials trained in this way inevitably came in conflict with the claims and demands of those prophets who, like Isaiah and Jeremiah, were deeply involved in the political affairs of the nation. We rarely encounter this kind of situation today, but the struggle during the Iranian revolution between the modernizing party and the Imams with their radical commitment to Islam may give some idea of what was involved.

With the loss of national independence much of the power of the monarchy and the court passed to the priesthood. In the texts which have survived from the period of the restoration the emphasis is on the study and observance of the laws. According to 1 and 2 Chronicles, our principal source, the scribe is now a teacher and a preacher, and what he teaches and preaches is the law. Whatever the political status of Ezra as emissary of the Persian government, it was his role as student, exponent, and teacher of the law which was important for the Chronicler. The purpose of his mission was to see that the 'law of the God of heaven' was known and observed in the province of Judah, indeed, in the entire satrapy 'Beyond the River' (Ezra 7: 25), and this goal involved an educational mission. The great assembly at which the law book was read by Ezra and explained by Levites (Neh. 8), whatever its historical character, probably reflects the actual practice of the Chronicler's own day; and the same could be said of his description of levitical scribes going from town to town giving instruction in the law (2 Chr. 17: 7-9).

By the time of Ben Sira the 'house of study' was a well-established institution in the cities and possibly also in the villages. Little as we know of the origins and early development of the synagogue, the indications are that from the earliest times it served as an educational centre as well as for prayer and worship. While 'profane' learning was certainly available in the Hellenistic cities for those Jews who had the means and the disposition to pursue it, the basic education was in Torah. Thus Josephus, a well educated man if no great thinker, informs us in his autobiography that 'while still a mere boy, about fourteen years old, I won universal applause for my love of letters; insomuch that the chief priests and the leading men of the city used constantly to come to me for precise information on some particular in our ordinances'. Another Pharisee, Paul, was also well versed in Torah and the various exegetical procedures then in use for the interpretation of Scripture. And while Josephus and Paul were hardly typical Pharisees, we are reminded that it was the Pharisees who, more than others, promoted Torah-learning among the people.

Many of the points made in this brief summary will be further developed and illustrated in subsequent chapters. Our main purpose will be to trace the two great streams of wisdom and law from their sources to the point where they flow together and eventually find their outlet in rabbinic writings and early Christian theology. The first and essential stage is, of course, the understanding of the relevant biblical texts themselves, and to these we now turn.

2

Education for Life

Proverbs: the book

Proverbs is a manual of didactic material, a source book of instruction containing several distinct compilations brought together and edited from a specific religious viewpoint some time during the period of the Second Temple. Despite the fact that some parts of the collection are attributed to specific individuals – e.g. Hezekiah's men (25: 1), Agur (30: 1), Lemuel (31: 1) – the work as a whole comes to us under the name of Solomon (1: 1). No one doubts, however, that this is a pseudonym, the result of a long-standing tradition of regarding Solomon as fountainhead of wisdom in all of its aspects including literary skill (1 Kgs. 4: 32). The attribution may, at any rate, serve to remind us that Proverbs contains genuinely ancient material, presenting us, in effect, with a cross-section of Israelite wisdom in its many historical phases over a period of several centuries.

The individual compositions or compilations in the book are fairly easy to disengage since almost all of them have titles. They may be set out as follows:

1. An instruction on wisdom and folly (1: 8 – 9: 18)
2. A 'Solomonic' collection of proverbs (10: 1 – 22: 16)
3. A collection entitled 'Sayings of the Wise' (22: 17 – 24: 22)
4. A supplementary collection with the same title (24: 23-34)
5. A second 'Solomonic' collection edited by Hezekiah's scribes (25: 1 – 29: 27)
6. Sayings of Agur (30: 1-9)
7. A collection of mostly numerical sayings (30: 10-33)
8. Sayings of Lemuel (31: 1-9)
9. Acrostic poem on the 'woman of substance' (31: 10-31)

It will be seen that the anthology is introduced as 'Proverbs of Solomon', which is understandable in view of the fact that the two collections of 'Solomonic' proverbs make up by far the largest part of the material in the book. It was noted in the previous chapter that the prologue (1: 2-7) presents the book as a manual for the education of the young. It concludes on an explicitly religious note with the reminder that

> The fear of Yahweh is the beginning of knowledge;
> fools despise wisdom and instruction. (1: 7)

If this comes from a later hand, as several commentators suggest, it would not be the only instance where the teaching of the sages has been brought firmly into line with Yahwistic piety (cf. Prov. 14: 27; Eccles. 12: 13; Job 28: 28). Alternating with the two major collections of proverbs are two instructions, the latter (22: 17 – 24: 34) being an Israelite adaptation of the Egyptian Wisdom of Amen-em-opet, as will be seen in greater detail at a later point. The final section, praising the good wife, is perhaps intended to correspond to the figure of the woman Wisdom presented in the first section. It was quite common in antiquity to round off a work in a way calculated to recall its opening.

That the book represents the effort of a Second Temple editor to bring together a cross-section of scribal wisdom covering a long period of time is apparent not only in the variety of the material included but also in the titles. Some of the parts are anonymous ('Sayings of the Wise'), some pseudonymous ('Proverbs of Solomon') and others are attributed to named individuals (Agur, Lemuel). Anonymity is normal in the ancient world. Pseudonymity arises in response to the need for legitimation by establishing links with a normative history; so, for example, the Pentateuch is attributed to Moses and Psalms to David. The practice of putting one's name to a book is attested only towards the end of the biblical period, the first instance we know of being Jesus ben Sira (Ecclus. 50: 27). While the sayings of Agur and Lemuel are the exception in Proverbs, by the time of the Mishnah (*c.* AD 200) it was common practice for sayings to be attributed to individual sages some of whom lived within the biblical period.

The proverb

It will be clear from both the title and content of the book that the proverb was the most characteristic form in which the sages and teachers of Israel gave instruction and expressed their understanding of human existence. While etymology is at best an imperfect guide to meaning, it may be worth noting that the Hebrew word *mashal* is associated by some with a word-group connoting 'rule' or 'power' and by others with the idea of 'comparison' or 'model'. Those who take the first line wish to emphasize the originally magical, incantatory and performative function of expressive language, while the alternative of 'model' or 'paradigm' will lead to stressing the representational and metaphoric function. If, however, we attend to the actual usage, we see that *mashal* can stand for a wide variety of literary forms in Proverbs and elsewhere in the Hebrew Bible. It can be used for a prophetic oracle (Num. 23: 7), a taunt (Jer. 24: 9) or an allegory (Ezek. 17: 2), and Job dismisses the teaching of his colleagues as 'proverbs of ashes' (Job 13: 12). In its characteristic form, however, it denotes a brief pointed saying, concrete in its imagery and general in its applicability, relating in some way to human character and conduct. This is the type that we find in the two long collections attributed to Solomon in the book.

If we look at proverbial material in different cultures, we may see some of the important roles that it can play. This will be the case even in such areas as the administration of justice where it can represent a kind of deposit of the accumulated wisdom of the past, a distillation of experience based on the observation of order, regularity and causality. Like traditional narrative or folktale, the corpus of proverbs in a so-called primitive society serves to transmit its collective values, thus forming the basis for an agreed pattern of behaviour over against which the conduct of the individual can be judged. We should therefore not be surprised to discover connections between proverbial wisdom and the early stages in the development of a legal tradition. Both appeal to precedent and base their authority on the transmitted wisdom of the past.

Quite a few proverbial expressions, of the short, pithy kind, can be found scattered throughout the Hebrew Bible. Examples such as the following could be found in practically any society: 'As the man is, so is his strength' (Judg. 8: 21), 'Out of the wicked comes forth wickedness' (1 Sam. 24: 13), 'Let not him who girds on his armour boast as he who puts it off' (1 Kgs. 20: 11), 'Like mother, like daughter' (Ezek. 16: 44). Others have a more specific historical point of reference: 'Like Nimrod, a mighty hunter before Yahweh' (Gen. 10: 9), 'Is Saul also among the prophets?' (1 Sam. 10: 11; 19: 24), 'Let them but ask counsel at Abel' (2 Sam. 20: 18). These last we recognize as proverbial sayings only because the context describes them as such. In other instances, especially in prophetic books, it is difficult to decide whether we are dealing with a genuine proverb or a rhetorical device. Examples would be Isaiah's 'Let us eat and drink, for tomorrow we die' (22: 13) or Jeremiah's question, 'What has straw in common with wheat?' (23: 28). A very rare case of a bicolon or two-member proverb comes from the time shortly before or after the fall of Jerusalem: 'The fathers have eaten sour grapes and the children's teeth are set on edge' (Jer. 31: 29; Ezek. 18: 2). Originally embodying the not uncommon complaint that the present generation is suffering from the mistakes of its predecessors, this proverb came to voice the accusation that God was using the Babylonians to punish his people for the sins of their ancestors.

When we turn from these popular proverbial sayings to the two major collections in Proverbs the difference is at once apparent. With very few exceptions, the proverbs they contain conform to a fixed type: a compact, two-member unit in verse, in the parallel arrangement typical of Hebrew poetry. The stylization and elaboration evident in this form do not suggest a popular folk origin. They are not popular but scholastic, and their intent is explicitly didactic. The bicolon (two-member) structure has the advantage of allowing the play of different kinds of relationship between the members without sacrificing that unity of form and content which is characteristic of the proverb. In some it is a case of a simple and explicit comparison:

> Like vinegar to the teeth, and smoke to the eyes,
>   so is the sluggard to those who send him.   (10: 26)

or

> Like the cold of snow in the time of harvest
>> is a faithful messenger to those who send him. (25: 13)

In others the comparison is implicit, and the proverb, therefore, a kind of extended metaphor:

> Iron sharpens iron,
>> and one man sharpens another. (27: 17)

A quite common form of juxtaposition occurs when we pass from the observation of regularity in nature to the moral order:

> The north wind brings rain,
>> and a backbiting tongue, angry looks. (25: 23)

or

> For lack of wood the fire goes out,
>> and where there is no whisperer, quarrelling ceases.
>>> (26: 20)

This type illustrates one of the basic goals of the sages in Israel and elsewhere in the ancient Near East: to bring human conduct into line with a cosmic law of regularity and order observable in the sequence of seasons, the movements of the heavenly bodies and the like. To be wise is, in a word, to live in conformity with the law of nature.

As in Hebrew poetry in general, the parallelism characteristic of these proverbs can be of different kinds. An example of synonymous parallelism would be:

> Even a fool who keeps silent is considered wise;
>> when he closes his lips, he is deemed intelligent. (17: 28)

— rather like the old Roman maxim, 'If you had kept quiet you would have passed for a philosopher'. Or, again:

> Even in laughter the heart is sad,
>> and the end of joy is grief. (14: 13)

— one of the very few instances in Proverbs which touch on the deeper, more baffling and paradoxical aspects of human existence. More common than these, however, is the kind which makes its point by contrast or antithesis:

> A wise son makes a glad father,
>> but a foolish son is a sorrow to his mother. (10: 1)

or

> Hatred stirs up strife,
>> but love covers all offences. (10: 12)

So prevalent is this type, in fact, that it serves to express what, if anything, is the central theme of this kind of 'sentence literature' — the antithesis between wisdom and folly or, in its later and specifically Israelite form, between righteousness and sin.

To take another, and final, example of the different ways in which these two-member proverbs are structured, we might look at the comparative type:

> Better is a dry morsel with quiet
>> than a house full of feasting with strife. (17: 1)

or

> It is better to live in a corner of the housetop
>> than in a house shared with a contentious woman.
>>> (21: 9)

This too corresponds to an important aspect of the sages' instruction: how to evaluate options and make wise choices. A more emphatic version is what we might call the *a fortiori* type:

> All a poor man's brothers hate him;
>> how much more do his friends go far from him! (19: 7)

or, at a deeper level:

> Sheol and Abaddon lie open before Yahweh,
>> how much more the hearts of men! (15: 11)

There are other types, but these may serve to illustrate the flexibility of the proverb as a didactic instrument.

The religious dimension

If we pass from a consideration of individual proverbs to the way they are presented in the book, we are confronted with the apparent lack of any principle of arrangement either in the two major collections or the book as a whole. This is all the more unfortunate in that structure is itself a vehicle of meaning. In several of the prophetic books, for example, and perhaps also in the arrangement of the prophetic corpus as a whole, there are indications of a concern to transmit a 'message' through a meaningful arrangement of the material. If we take another glance at the table of contents laid out above we may detect an *artistic* arrangement of the several parts somewhat in the following manner:

Instruction (1: 8 − 9: 18)	Instruction (22: 17 − 24: 34)
Proverbs (10: 1 − 22: 16)	Proverbs (25-29)
Sayings of Agur (30: 1-14)	Sayings of Lemuel (31: 1-9)
Numerical Sayings (30: 15-33)	Acrostic poem (31: 10-31)

Whether the arrangement is anything more than formal, however, is difficult to say. In the proverb collections, likewise, indications of orderly arrangement are few and far between. Some are grouped on the catchword principle (e.g. gold, 25: 11-12), or according to type (e.g. simile, 25: 11-14, 18-20). Sayings contrasting the righteous and the wicked tend to cluster (e.g. 10: 20-32; 11: 4-11; 12: 2-7), but there does not seem to be any overall systematic order in their presentation.

Some progress may, nevertheless, be made along a different line of enquiry. We note that the book contains several examples of two variants of the same saying, sometimes in the same collection. One instance, a particularly graphic one, occurs in one of the two instructions:

> The sluggard says, 'There is a lion in the road!
> There is a lion in the streets!' (26: 13, cf. 22: 13)

− certainly as good an excuse as any for not getting out of bed in the morning. Most of these (e.g. 14: 12 = 16: 25; 18: 8 = 26: 22; 19: 12 = 20: 2) have no particular significance except to remind us that the collections have undergone extensive editing. But there are one or two which suggest a deliberate modification made from a specifically religious point of view:

> The crucible is for silver, and the furnace is for gold,
>> and a man is judged by his praise. (27: 21)

> The crucible is for silver, and the furnace is for gold,
>> and Yahweh tries hearts. (17: 3)

The former is in accord with the ethos of the old wisdom according to which everyone must pass the test of public approval. The latter introduces a quite different criterion of evaluation which in fact calls the older wisdom into question. Even clearer is the saying which describes the teaching of the sages as a fountain of life (13: 14, cf. 16: 22), when we compare it with the following:

> The fear of Yahweh is a fountain of life,
>> that one may avoid the snares of death. (14: 27)

It seems reasonable to conclude that an early corpus of gnomic material, embodying the kind of prudential, religiously neutral, and sometimes even simply opportunistic ethic found in Egyptian instructions, has been given a Yahwistic 'baptism'. The difference in attitude between certain proverbs and sets of proverbs will be seen more clearly if we take the example of the acquisition and use of wealth, a subject of great interest to the sages. In some proverbs poverty is simply a misfortune:

> A rich man's wealth is his strong city;
>> the poverty of the poor is their ruin.
>>> (10: 15, cf. 18: 11)

Others offer advice on how to get rich:

> Wealth hastily gotten will dwindle;
>> he who gathers little by little will increase it. (13: 11)

and remind us that money is the best way to make friends and influence people:

> The poor is disliked even by his neighbour;
>> the rich has many friends. (14: 20, cf. 19: 4, 7)

We are also reminded that a little greasing of the palm may at times be the answer to a particular problem:

> A bribe is like a magic stone in the eyes of him who
>> gives it;
> wherever he turns he prospers. (17: 8)

or

> A gift in secret averts anger;
>> a bribe in the bosom strong wrath. (21: 14)

Informed by a quite different ethos are those proverbs which inculcate a basic distrust of wealth:

> Riches do not profit in the day of wrath,
>> but righteousness delivers from death. (11: 4)

> He who trusts in his riches will wither,
>> but the righteous will flourish like a green leaf. (11: 28)

Even clearer is the condemnation of bribery, especially when used to pervert the course of justice:

> A wicked man accepts a bribe from the bosom
>> to pervert the ways of justice. (17: 23)

We are reminded of the stipulation in the oldest collection of Israelite laws, the so-called Covenant Code: 'You shall take no bribe, for a bribe blinds officials and subverts the cause of the righteous'. (Ex. 23: 8). By the simple substitution of 'wise' for 'officials' the Deuteronomic law (Deut. 16: 19) has brought the sapiential tradition of Israel to bear on the administration of justice. In brief, it seems that these variants point to a transformation of the old international scribal tradition under the influence of the religion of Yahweh and its representatives.

This process of adaptation and indigenization can also be detected in the second instruction in the book (Prov. 22: 17 – 24: 22) which has numerous parallels with the Egyptian Instruction of

Amen-em-opet, a high-ranking scribe from about the seventh century BC. This work stands out in the corpus of Egyptian didactic writing for its high moral tone and concern for the powerless, which would certainly help to explain its appeal to a devout Israelite sage. The similarity in tone, in theme, and even at times in language can be seen in the following example:

> Guard thyself against robbing the oppressed,
> and against overbearing the disabled. (Chapter 2)

> Do not rob the poor because he is poor,
>   or crush the afflicted at the gate. (Prov. 22: 22)

or even more specifically:

> Do not carry off the landmark at the boundaries of
>   the arable land,
> nor disturb the position of the measuring cord;
> be not greedy for a cubit of land,
> nor encroach upon the boundaries of a widow . . .
> Guard against encroaching upon the boundaries of
>   the fields
> lest a terror carry thee off. (Chapter 6)

> Remove not the ancient landmark
>   which your fathers have set. (Prov. 22: 28)
> Do not remove an ancient landmark
>   or enter the fields of the fatherless;
> for their Redeemer is strong;
>   he will plead their cause against you. (Prov. 23: 10–11)

The adaptation involved recognition of Yahweh as upholder of the moral order (22: 23; 24: 17–18) and the inculcation of the 'fear of Yahweh' — meaning a way of life appropriate to the cult of Yahweh — as the epitome of order and morality (23: 17; 24: 1). It was also to be expected that the ethical teaching of the instruction should be reinforced by referring to the contrasting fates of the righteous and the wicked (24: 15–16).

The evidence for adaptation and development within the book leads to the conclusion that collections of proverbs expressing the common ethos of the scribal schools have been modified and sup-

plemented by religious teachers after the Babylonian exile. Characteristic of the latter is the fear of Yahweh as the epitome of the
moral life (e.g. 10: 27), the belief in Yahweh as sustainer of the
moral order (e.g. 10: 3), the description of certain kinds of conduct
as an 'abomination to Yahweh' (e.g. 11: 1, 20; cf. the 'abomination
laws' in Deut. 17: 1 etc.), the use of specifically religious categories
like sin, prayer, and sacrifice, and the contrast, monotonously
repeated, between the fate of the righteous and that of the wicked.
A further conclusion is that among the devout scribes of the Second
Temple period the contrast between the righteous and the wicked
tended to displace the contrasting portraits of the wise man and the
fool in the older wisdom teaching. Since this is the starting point
for all later developments, it might be well to examine it more
closely before going any further.

The ethic of the sages

The basic assumption of the sapiential tradition in the Near East
was that wisdom is a quality of life which can be learned. Hence
the emphasis in Proverbs on discipline and education, apparent in
the numerous allusions to wise or foolish sons (e.g. 10: 1; 15: 20;
19: 13). Hence also the standard apostrophe 'my son' in the proverbs
and instructions referring to the disciple or student. The most
important item on the curriculum was not theology but decorum
and etiquette, and especially the prudent use of speech:

> A prudent man conceals his knowledge,
>   but fools proclaim their folly. (12: 23)

> If one answers before he has listened,
>   it is his folly and shame. (18: 13)

> Do you see a man who is hasty in his words?
>   there is more hope for a fool than for him. (29: 30)

This is precisely the kind of injunction which occurs routinely in
Egyptian instructions and such Mesopotamian texts as the Words of
Ahiqar. Contrasted with the wise person who is cool and temperate
in speech, knows the virtues of silence and, in Hamlet's words, is

not 'passion's slave', is the 'hot man' who takes no advice, has not
acquired the habit of listening and speaks out of season:

> A man without self-control
>   is like a city broken into and left without walls.
>
>   (25: 28)

It also follows that one must choose one's company with care,
for

> He who walks with wise men becomes wise,
>   but the companion of fools will suffer harm, (13: 20)

or, as Plutarch put it in his treatise *On the Education of Children*,
'if you live with a lame man you will learn to limp'. The prudent
man will also govern his household with firmness and discretion.
When going about his business, and especially when away from
home, he will eschew the company of women and avoid visiting
prostitutes. In the presence of higher authority he will assume an
appropriate attitude of respect, not speaking out of turn, not being
too forward (e.g. 25: 6-7). And he will act in this way not just to
avoid humiliation, or in the hope of advancing his career, but because
it is the appropriate thing to do in those circumstances.

It would be easy to criticize this teaching as at best pedestrian
and at worst complaisant and ethically insensitive on a whole range
of issues. While it frequently enjoins attention to the rights of the
poor and disadvantaged, as do the Egyptian instructions, it simply
takes for granted a hierarchical and feudal society in which advance-
ment depends on wealth and influence in high places. Its frequently
derogatory and petulant attitude to women (e.g. 19: 13; 21: 9, 19;
25: 24; 27: 15-16) is by no means peculiar to Israel, but that will
do little to alleviate the distasteful impression which it conveys.
We have to remind ourselves that, with the exception of the advice
of the queen mother to Lemuel (31: 1-9), this is literature written
by men and for men. So that even where women are praised it will
not always seem to us to be for the right reasons — witness the
rather 'bourgeois' portrait of the 'woman of substance' with its
catalogue of managerial skills (31: 10-31). Its educational theory,
if we may call it that, has too much of the 'spare the rod, spoil the

child' approach to gain wide endorsement today (e.g. 10: 13; 13: 24; 19: 18; 22: 15; 29: 15). And, in general, much of it seems to be aimed at getting on, or sometimes just getting by, in life.

While such a negative criticism would certainly hold for some of the material which we are surveying, it would not do justice to the ethos of the scribal schools as a whole, either in Israel or elsewhere in the Near East. We must bear in mind that it started out as strictly vocational instruction, restricted to a very small class of aspirants to public office. Its inculcation of the virtues of truth, honesty, and self-control in public life has nothing to fear from comparison with standards which have come to be accepted, or tolerated, in our contemporary societies. In its search for order behind the apparent chaos of experience, its endeavour to teach how to discriminate between options and make reasonable choices, its delineation of human types, it laid the basis for a genuine social ethic applicable outside the class to which it was first addressed. As such, its contribution to public life in Israel has a highly distinctive quality which should not be ignored.

The instruction

So far we have dealt almost exclusively with the proverb as a didactic instrument used by the teachers and sages. The reason is that the proverb was taken to be the basic unit of instruction in the schools, and therefore one of the principal activities of the sages was the collecting, arranging, and evaluating of proverbs (e.g. Eccles. 12: 9). But the sages used a wide variety of literary forms apart from the the proverb, each one of which would require careful and detailed treatment. For our present purpose, it will be sufficient to note the more important of these, with special attention to their use as didactic tools and the connections which can be shown to exist between them.

From ancient Egypt several complete or fragmentary examples of the instruction have survived covering a vast period of time with relatively little evidence of development. Purporting to be advice from a pharaoh in his declining years to the crown prince (e.g. the Instruction of Meri-ka-re), or from a vizier to his son who is to succeed him in office (e.g. Ptah-hotep in the third millennium BC), or by a lower echelon administrator to his son (e.g. Amen-em-opet), these admonitions are cast in direct address, make frequent use of the imperative, and provide motivation for the faithful implementation of the precepts. Remarkably stable as it is, this genre was favoured by moralists and philosophers in Late Antiquity, flourished in the Middle Ages, and passed into modern European literature as a well-known literary convention, e.g., in the plays of Shakespeare.

Beginning as early as the United Monarchy, the instruction was adopted by Israelite sages and continued in use down into the Second Temple. In Proverbs the section entitled 'Sayings of Lemuel' (31: 1-9) approximates most closely to the Egyptian type in that it purports to be a charge delivered by the queen mother to her son who is either preparing to reign or has just begun to do so. It is therefore presented explicitly as a 'mirror for princes' and contains the usual admonitions to avoid sexual irregularity, drunkenness, and injustice. As noted earlier, another section (22: 17 – 24: 22) appears to be modelled on the Instruction of Amen-em-opet and, like the latter, is divided into thirty units. These, however, are much shorter than the chapters of the Egyptian text and usually run to no more than four lines. The structure is simple: an admonition in the imperative in the first couplet and appropriate motivation in the second. In a later chapter we shall see that this pattern – imperative or prohibitive with motivation – occurs in the Decalogue and in other types of legal enactment (see p. 92). There are also longer units in this instruction in which the imperative–motivation unit has dissolved into something rather different: a graphic example of the consequences of acting in a certain way. Take, for example, the case of drunkenness:

> Who has woe? Who has sorrow?
>> Who has strife? Who has complaining?
> Who has wounds without cause?
>> Who has redness of eyes?
> Those who tarry long over wine,
>> those who go to try mixed wine.
> Do not look at wine when it is red,
>> when it sparkles in the cup and goes down smoothly.

> At the last it bites like a serpent,
>> and stings like an adder.
> Your eyes will see strange things,
>> and your mind utter perverse things.
> You will be like one who lies down in the midst of
>> the sea,
>> like one who lies on the top of the mast.
> 'They struck me,' you will say, 'but I was not hurt;
>> they beat me, but I did not feel it.
> When shall I awake?
>> I will seek another drink.' (23: 29–35)

Even in its most compressed form, the instruction differs from the typical proverb in its addiction to the imperative. There are, nevertheless, significant links between the two types which can best be illustrated by an example. The proverbial aphorism, 'pride comes before a fall', simply states compendiously a causal connection on the basis of many individual observations. The instructional counterpart would be something like, 'know your place' or 'don't step out of line'. The proverbial form occurs in the Solomonic collections:

> When pride comes, then comes disgrace;
>> but with the humble is wisdom. (11: 2)

or, alternatively,

> Pride goes before destruction,
>> and haughty spirit before a fall. (16: 18)

In the second Solomonic collection the same point is made in the form characteristic of the instruction:

> Do not put yourself forward in the king's presence
>> or stand in the place of the great;
> for it is better to be told, 'Come up here,'
>> than to be put lower in the presence of the prince.
>> (25: 6–7)

This will bring to mind the gospel passage (Lk. 14: 7–11) which is presented as a parable of Jesus but is in fact an instruction rounded off with a proverbial saying. It may be set out as follows:

From exaltation to humiliation

When you are invited by any one to a marriage feast, do not sit down in a place of honour, lest a more eminent man than you be invited by him; and he who invited you both will come, and say to you, 'Give place to this man,' and then you will begin with shame to take the lowest place.

From humiliation to exaltation

But when you are invited, go and sit in the lowest place, so that when your host comes he may say to you, 'Friend, go up higher'; then you will be honoured in the presence of all who sit at table with you.

Paradox and reversal

For every one who exalts himself will be humbled, and he who humbles himself will be exalted.

The brief instruction in Proverbs has here been expanded into two contrasting units to allow for the kind of paradoxical proverbial saying which seems to have been characteristic of the teaching of Jesus (see Mk. 8: 36-7; 10: 31; Lk. 17: 33).

This facility in transposing the same message from one genre to another can be observed in other gospel sayings. To take only one further example, the proverbial saying, 'He who tends a fig tree will eat its fruit' (Prov. 27: 18), appears to have suggested the particular form of an oracle of judgment in Jeremiah (8: 13) where Yahweh comes to harvest figs from his fig tree – meaning Israel – and finds none. In the gospels the same figure appears both in the form of a parable (Lk. 13: 6-9) and as the prophetic, symbolic action of the cursing of the barren fig tree (Mt. 21: 18-22).

Returning once again to Proverbs, we note that the first section also contains examples of the instruction, here too of the fairly short type introduced by the conventional apostrophe 'my son . . . '. Many, however, have been expanded in different ways as, for example, with rhetorical questions (e.g. 6: 27-8), vivid description (e.g. 7: 6-23), autobiographical reflections (4: 4-9) or perorations (7: 24-7). The advice given is not significantly different from that of the Egyptian sages: avoidance of bad company and of prostitutes, keeping the passions under control, performance of duties to the neighbour and to God. The section also contains portraits of the sluggard, the devious character, the seductive prostitute, of a kind encountered in cautionary tales from all ages. The most remarkable feature, however, is the public address of Wisdom to the foolish and uninstructed (1: 20-33; 8: 1-31; 9: 1-6). Because of its importance for later developments, this will be examined in a subsequent chapter.

Other genres

Among the principal literary forms used by the sages, then, were the proverb and the instruction, and it is these which make up the bulk of the material in Proverbs. But effective teaching calls for a variety of techniques whether to help the memory, arouse curiosity or stimulate the mind to make certain associations or draw conclusions from stated premisses. Acrostic compositions, like the poem about the good wife at the end of the book (31: 10-13), facilitated memorizing and perhaps, in addition, gave their authors the satisfying sense of making an all-inclusive statement. Though not conducive to a high level of poetic expression, they occur with some frequency in liturgical hymns (e.g. Pss. 9-10; 111-12; 145; Lam. 1-4). Better attested is the numerical saying which announces a specific number of items and then goes on to enumerate them. In some respects this type of saying resembles the list or onomasticon, familiar to the Egyptian and Sumero-akkadian scribal traditions, which served to classify and order the phenomena of nature and therefore could be used in teaching subjects like geography, zoology, and botany. While such educational material has not come down to us from Israel of the biblical period, something of the method is reflected in the tradition of Solomon's encyclopaedic wisdom alluded to earlier.

The examples of the genre in Proverbs are somewhat different in that the emphasis is really on human conduct even when they deal in what used to be called 'natural history'. Thus, the four small but wise creatures in Prov. 30: 24-28 are chosen as apt to teach valuable lessons in social living:

> Four things on earth are small,
>> but they are exceedingly wise:
> the ants are a people not strong,
>> yet they provide their food in the summer;
> the badgers are a people not mighty,
>> yet they make their homes in the rocks;
> the locusts have no king,
>> yet all of them march in rank;
> the lizard you can take in your hands,
>> yet it is in kings' palaces.

A negative lesson could also be learned from the leech and its suckers, if that is the meaning of the obscure term in Prov. 30: 15. Arrangement in numerical sequence has an obviously mnemonic function and has been used to teach children since time immemorial. One thinks of the children's song at the end of the Passover *seder*:

> Who knows one? I know one.
> One is our God in heaven and on earth.
>
> Who knows two? I know two.
> Two are the tablets of the covenant;
> One is our God in heaven and on earth

and so on in progressive and cumulative sequence up to the thirteen attributes of God. Many other examples of the use of this technique in secular instruction and religious catechesis could be given. The arrangements of laws in sets of ten (to be counted on the ten fingers?) may also have had the same function.

A special case would be the type of saying based on two numbers, one higher than the other — what might be called the progressive numerical saying. Starting from the common practice of indicating approximation by numbers in sequence ('two or three'), this type is stylized according to the verse parallelism characteristic of Hebrew poetry. Together with other stylistic features, it appears to have been taken over from Canaanite poetic convention, as the following example from the Ugaritic Baal-cycle suggests:

> Two sacrifices Baal hates,

three, the Rider on the Clouds:
a sacrifice of shame,
a sacrifice of meanness,
and a sacrifice of the lewdness of handmaids

— referring, no doubt, to irregularities and abuses in the practice of the sacrificial cult the precise nature of which is no longer apparent. With this we may compare Prov. 6: 16-19:

There are six things which Yahweh hates,
seven which are an abomination to him:
haughty eyes, a lying tongue,
and hands that shed innocent blood,
a heart that devises wicked plans,
feet that make haste to run to evil,
a false witness who breathes out lies,
and a man who sows discord among brothers.

Most of our examples are concentrated in the seventh section of the book (Prov. 30: 10-33) and in Ben Sira. Almost all of the combinations between one-two (Ps. 62: 11-12; Job 33: 14) and nine-ten (Ecclus. 25: 7) are attested, the majority of them at the lower end. While the intent is clearly mnemonic, some of them have a riddle-like quality, as if to tease the mind into considering realities below the level of everyday observation. While not entirely characteristic of the genre, the following example seems to be of this kind:

Three things are too wonderful for me;
four I do not understand:
the way of an eagle in the sky,
the way of a serpent on a rock,
the way of a ship on the high seas,
and the way of a man with a maiden.
(Prov. 30:18-19)

In this instance the sequence has the effect of stressing the fourth 'way', in the sense that the mysterious element in the first three provides the clue to the meaning. In other words, the common element in the first three, a mysterious form of propulsion, leads into a consideration of the deep mystery of sexual attraction. For the Hebrew reader the point would have been reinforced by a cunning play on words, since the word *derek* (way) also has a sexual connotation — as, for example, in Prov. 31: 3 where 'ways' is parallel with 'virility'.

It will be inevitable to think of a connection of some sort between this kind of saying and the riddle which also, not uncommonly, deals with sexual matters. While no collection of Hebrew riddles has survived, it is explicitly stated that their composition and solution fell within the competence of the sages (Prov. 1: 6). In this respect, as in others, Solomon was the model sage. We hear of the Queen of Sheba coming to test him with riddles, and it is quite conceivable that a collection of riddles originally stood at this point of the narra-tive. In the midrash she is transformed into the demon Lilith and her riddles, like that of the Sphinx, are potentially fatal. Josephus too records contests of this kind between Solomon and foreign sages (*Antiquities* 8: 146–9). Riddles were used in Israel, as in other cultures, for many purposes. The Hebrew term (*ḥidah*) is used for certain liturgical compositions (Ps. 49: 5; 78: 2) and for the dark and sometimes ambiguous utterances of a prophet (Num. 12: 8; Ezek. 17: 2; Hab. 2: 6). In both cases there is the sense that, at its deepest levels, human existence inevitably has a riddle-like quality about it.

At the level of popular usage the riddle was, of course, a means of entertainment, being an especially popular feature at banquets. The riddling that went on at Samson's wedding feast is the only example which has come down to us, but provides a good instance of both context and form. It was a genuine contest, with a consider-able wager at stake, the riddles being propounded in a thinly con-cealed atmosphere of hostility and menace. Samson's initial riddle:

> Out of the eater came something to eat.
> Out of the strong came something sweet.   (Judg. 14: 14)

is also typical in that, like several of the Anglo-Saxon riddles, the surface meaning served to disguise a deeper meaning, often of a sexual nature. In the hands of the sages this universally popular form of diversion came to serve a didactic purpose, presenting the well-known in new ways, redefining the familiar, stretching and sharpening the mind of the student.

The dialogue, debate or dispute could also serve as a medium of instruction, especially for the formulation and solution of problems of a speculative nature. Since the biblical examples of Job and Abraham's dialogue with God over the fate of Sodom (Gen. 18) take us well beyond any scholastic curriculum, they should be classified as speculative rather than didactic wisdom, and as such they will be considered in a subsequent chapter. Confessional and autobiographical passages, generally spoken under an assumed identity, belong to the same class. Their best representatives are the Egyptian instructions and the 'royal testament' of Qoheleth. Other non-narrative genres sometimes listed as sapiential, the didactic poem for example, simply illustrate the fact that the sages could make use of practically any literary form when it served their purpose to do so.

Sapiential narrative

We are on much less certain ground when we go on to ask what use the sages made of narrative for didactic purposes. The parable is an obvious place to start, but presents us at once with a problem of definition. Apart from the fact that there is no Hebrew term which clearly designates this genre, our perception of what a parable is and how it works tends to be determined by the gospel parables which happen to be the best known but may not be the most typical. A satisfactory solution to this problem would require a broad comparative study which cannot be undertaken here. Parables attributed to Jesus, and to other Jewish sages of Late Antiquity, at least demonstrate that there is an affinity between the proverb and the parable similar to that between the proverb and the instruction which we have noted earlier. Thus, the gospel parables which compare the Kingdom of Heaven to a field, a net, or a batch of yeast, may be read as narrative parallels to the simile-proverbs discussed earlier in this chapter. And, in general, the vivid and concrete language of Hebrew aphorisms would make it relatively easy to develop their narrative nucleus in parabolic form. To take an example at random:

> He who meddles in a quarrel not his own
> is like one who takes a passing dog by the ears.
>
> (Prov. 26: 17)

could, without much difficulty, be transposed into a brief and vivid parable.

As far as we can judge from the surviving literature, the sages of Israel seem to have made relatively little use of the parable for purposes of instruction. The story of the rich man who stole the poor man's ewe lamb, told by Nathan to David after the latter had committed adultery with Bathsheba and murdered her husband (2 Sam. 12: 1-6), illustrates very well one essential characteristic of parables, namely, their capacity to involve the reader. In its present context, however, it is attributed to a seer rather than a sage. The story which the wise woman of Tekoa told David about her two sons one of whom, having killed the other, is in immediate danger of death (2 Sam. 14: 4-7), is a skilful fictionalization of the situation in David's family but no parable. The same must be said of the prophet's story, told to king Ahab, about losing a prisoner of war (1 Kgs. 20: 35-43). Other passages which are sometimes adduced as examples are the unproductive vineyard (Isa. 5: 1-2) and the sensible farmer (Isa. 28: 23-6). While they share with many of the parables of Jesus the scenario of the countryside, they are not really narrative and occur, significantly, in a prophetic book.

More clearly didactic in purpose is the fable, understood as a short story featuring animals or inanimate things as actors, which is designed to teach a lesson or make a point. The animal fable, of the kind favoured by Aesop, seems to have been very popular among the Sumerians as far back as the third millennium BC. Since the juxtaposition of animal and human types easily brings into play both the comic and the cruel, the fable also lends itself to satire. An extremely brief example is the answer sent by a king of Israel in the early eighth century BC to a king of Judah who had challenged him to do battle:

> A thistle on Lebanon sent to a cedar on Lebanon, saying, 'Give your daughter to my son for a wife'; and a wild beast of Lebanon passed by and trampled down the thistle. (2 Kgs. 14: 9)

More extended in length is the fable of the convocation of trees which assembled to choose a king and which ended with the bramble putting himself forward for election (Judg. 9: 7–15). In its present context it serves as a savagely effective satire on the pretensions of the usurper Abimelech and perhaps also on monarchy in general.

While these are the only examples of the fable in the Hebrew Bible, we have no reason to doubt that the genre was popular in ancient Israel and in use in the schools. Animal and plant fables occur in the teaching of the legendary Ahiqar known to the Jewish colony which settled at Elephantine on the Upper Nile in the fifth century BC. Fables also seem to have been used to teach natural history in Mesopotamia, to judge by extant examples such as the Babylonian 'Dispute between the Tamarisk and the Date Palm'. No such example has, however, survived from ancient Israel.

Scholars have been debating for a long time as to whether certain longer narratives in the Hebrew Bible and the Apocrypha can be placed within the 'wisdom movement' or have at least been subjected to 'wisdom influences'. What this presumably means is that in certain cases the *primary* intent in composing a narrative was to make a point or teach a lesson rather than, for example, to record history or entertain. Unfortunately, this is practically impossible to determine with a reasonable degree of probability. In the previous chapter it was suggested that the court history dealing with the succession to David's throne (2 Sam. 11–20; 1 Kgs. 1–2) embodies themes and language characteristic of the sages. Much the same can be said of the structurally similar story of the Garden of Eden (Gen. 2: 4 – 3: 24). Its learned use of mythological themes, skilful dialogue and profound exploration of the limits of human resources suggest the same origin. It may be noted, in confirmation, that mythological themes abound in writings which are explicitly sapiential: the first man (Job 15: 7-8), the tree of life (Prov. 3: 18), the rebellion of heavenly beings (Job 4: 18; 15: 15; 25: 5), monsters of the deep (e.g. Job 3: 8; 7: 12; 9: 13) and many others. It is therefore by no means implausible that the sages of Israel took over well-known mythic narrative themes for their own purposes.

Since the principal milieu of the scribes and sages in early Israel was the court, it is not surprising that several narratives which bear their imprint have a court setting. The obvious example is the succession history, discussed earlier, which features a contest of sages and pits the professional wisdom of Ahithophel against a providence which guides Solomon to the throne against all human odds. Less obvious, though no less suggestive, is the story of Joseph in Genesis (37-50). The novelistic character of this narrative stands out quite clearly in contrast to those dealing with the earlier ancestors, and it differs from them in other significant respects as well. The deeper levels of meaning are revealed not through visions and theophanies but in dreams – those of Joseph himself (37: 5-11), the pharaoh (41: 1-8) and his servants (40: 5-19). Joseph rises to prominence at the Egyptian court because he is recognized to be 'a man discreet and wise' (41: 33, 39), and his wisdom includes skill in the interpretation of dreams and in divination (41: 15; 44: 15). This wisdom, however, is a divine gift in reward for his fidelity (39: 2-3, 21-3) demonstrated in his rejection of a married woman's advances (39: 6-18). As in the court history of David, the action is controlled from beginning to end by a hidden providence. As Joseph explains to his brothers:

> As for you, you meant evil against me; but God meant it for good, to bring it about that many people should be kept alive, as they are today. (50: 20)

The entire story breathes the atmosphere of the sages and bears comparison with other biblical narratives in which similar themes appear, e.g., the court tales in Dan. 1-6 which we shall consider in Chapter 6.

Much of the action in Esther also takes place at court, this time during the Persian period. The principal characters, moreover, are idealized and paradigmatic: Esther herself is a woman of beauty, wisdom, and courage; Mordecai, her cousin and guardian, is a wise and prudent counsellor; and Haman, descendant of the hated Agag, is the archetypal enemy of the Jewish people. The account of Haman's undoing, ending with his death on the gibbet which he had prepared for Mordecai, provides a perfect illustration of the sages' teaching on retribution. So the author has certainly made use of procedures and themes familiar to the teachers of wisdom. Since, however, the story in its present form is meant to explain the origins of the festival of Purim, it can hardly be described as didactic in the sense of teaching important lessons for the conduct of life. The militantly nationalistic tone is also unparalleled in other sapiential compositions known to us and would lead us to look elsewhere for its origins.

Much the same problem – that of genre or category – confronts us in reading Judith, one of the additional books in the Greek Bible, and here too only a brief comment will be possible. The story relates how the Assyrian king Nebuchadnezzar sent his general Holofernes on a punitive expedition against his rebellious subjects in Phoenicia and Palestine. Israel being the only province to resist, Holofernes took counsel with his vassals and was advised by Achior, the Ammonite leader, that the Jews were invincible as long as they took care to observe their laws. Disregarding this advice, he laid siege to Bethulia, a town in the Central Highlands which blocked his advance on Jerusalem. After cutting off the town's water supply, Holofernes reduced the inhabitants to such straits that they demanded of Uzziah their leader that he capitulate. At this point Judith, a wealthy and devout widow, prevailed on Uzziah to allow her to execute a cunningly devised plan to seduce the Assyrian general, assassinate him and thus throw his entire army into disarray. The plan succeeded, and the story comes to a climax of gothic horror with Judith pulling the general's severed head from her bag and showing it to her compatriots.

Those who argue that this narrative is sapiential or didactic can point to the portrayal of Judith as a model of wisdom (8: 29; 11: 20-3) combined with piety and, indeed, since Judith means 'Jewess', as *the* model of Israelite womanhood. While this is correct as far as it goes, it does not help very much in determining with any precision what the story is really about. That the Babylonian Nebuchadnezzar is described as king of the Assyrians will remind us of his role in the court tales in Daniel 1-6 where he stands for Antiochus IV, ruler of the Syrian kingdom of the Seleucids. This will be confirmed by references in Judith to the cult of the divinized king (3: 8; 6: 2), the plundering and destruction of temples (3: 8; 4: 1-2 etc.), the fact that Israel alone resisted the tyrant (3-4) and the similarity between the fate of Holofernes and that of the Seleucid general Nicanor (1 Macc. 7: 43–50). Following the lead of these different clues scattered throughout the book, we should read it as a celebration of the Maccabean triumph written not long after Daniel. Judith herself, then, would embody the kind of assiduous piety illustrated in Daniel. She prays at the proper times (11: 17; 13: 3), fasts (8: 6), observes sabbath (10: 2), the food laws (12: 2–4), tithing and firstfruits (11: 12–15) together with the prescribed ritual ablutions (12: 7–9). In acting thus she demonstrates a God-given wisdom which enables her to save her people. If this means that the book is sapiential or didactic, we would probably have to say the same of almost all the religious narrative literature which has survived from the Graeco-Roman period.

We may conclude, then, that the further we get away from the basic instruments of instruction in the scribal schools the less useful is the term 'sapiential' as a descriptive label. This is true of Judith and also of Tobit, another book in the Greek Bible which deals with exemplary conduct and its reward. But even without these borderline cases, enough has been said to establish the remarkable range and versatility of the instruction which the sages of Israel offered.

3

God and the Moral Order

The link between act and consequence

One of the ways in which the sages of Israel, and of the ancient world in general, attempted to make sense of human existence was to postulate an intrinsic connection between act and consequence and thereby lay the basis for a morally significant life. The observation that pride leads to disaster (e.g. Prov. 11: 2; 16: 18; 18: 12), or that laziness generally leads to poverty (e.g. Prov. 10: 4; 20: 13; 21: 25), made on the basis of experience, was intended to suggest obvious consequences for the moral life. While this kind of teaching does not amount to a 'doctrine of retribution', it can too easily be applied in doctrinaire fashion and be made to serve as an instrument of moral evaluation. We are all familiar with the point of view that the poor owe their condition to laziness; a conclusion which is true in some instances but inadequate as a general explanation of poverty.

One result of the assimilation of this 'old wisdom' to the specifically religious content of Israel's life as a community was that the act–consequence link gave rise to serious theological problems. Faith in Yahweh entailed the conviction that he presided over and validated the moral order as lord and judge of his people. The intrinsic connection between human deed and its consequences was not thereby abandoned, but the religious dimension made it easier to think in terms of reward and punishment flowing from the divine administration of justice. This can be seen in Solomon's prayer at the dedication of the temple, a passage generally attributed to a Deuteronomic author of the late monarchy or exilic age:

> If a man sins against his neighbour and is made to take an oath . . .
> then hear thou in heaven, and act, and judge thy servants, con-
> demning the guilty by bringing his conduct upon his own head,

and vindicating the righteous by rewarding him according to his righteousness. (1 Kgs. 8: 31-2)

The implication is that good and bad actions are not always seen to have their appropriate consequences, and that therefore the moral order – in this case respect for oaths – demands the intervention of God as judge. It followed that any threat to the moral order risked calling into question either the power or the justice of God.

These implications are apparent in the religiously inspired aphorisms of the two large collections in Proverbs. The idea of an *intrinsic* link between act and consequence is still detectable – for example, in proverbs which speak of sowing and reaping (26: 27; 28: 10) – but the monotonous contrast between the fate of the righteous and that of the wicked is based on specifically religious premisses. Expressions like the following could hardly arise out of observation and experience alone:

> No ill befalls the righteous,
> but the wicked are filled with trouble. (12: 21)

or

> The righteous has enough to satisfy his appetite,
> but the belly of the wicked suffers want. (13: 25)

Even less could the contention that the wicked come to an untimely end while the righteous live out their days (e.g. Prov. 10: 27). The same view is maintained in the more developed and speculative teaching in Prov. 1-9, where the motive-clauses frequently attached to the instructions suggest that religious observance ('the fear of Yahweh') is rewarded with long life and wellbeing (e.g. 3: 1-2, 9-10).

Since the language of prayer in Israel addresses God as all-powerful ruler and judge, we would expect to find something like the same point of view in Psalms which, like Proverbs, is a compilation dating in its final form to the late Second Temple period. The first psalm recapitulates an important aspect of scribal piety by contrasting the fate of the wicked with that of the righteous. It concludes:

> For Yahweh knows the way of the righteous,
>> but the way of the wicked will perish.

Nor is this the only instance of affinity with the wisdom of the scribes. Two other compositions — Pss. 49 and 78 — are presented as proverbial discourse and riddle and deal, in different ways, with the mystery of evil and its consequences. Among psalms composed in the acrostic form — discussed briefly in the previous chapter — we also find this contrast between religious observance and impiety (e.g. Ps. 119). The frequent prayer for vengeance on the wicked, unpalatable as it may be to modern sensitivities, is motivated by the absolute theological necessity for the divine justice to be seen and acknowledged (e.g. Ps. 58). Many of the psalms of individual lamentation presuppose that sickness and other ills are the direct consequence of divine judgment following on sin, even inadvertent sin (e.g. Ps. 90: 7-8). In some of these hymns a morally rational worldview, in which virtue is always rewarded and wickedness always punished, is maintained in defiance of experience:

> I have been young, and now am old;
>> yet I have not seen the righteous forsaken
>> or his children begging bread. (Ps. 37: 25)

A similar claim would be made by Job's friends in an effort to get him to confess to wrongdoing in some way commensurate with his sufferings and thus maintain the traditional rationale of evil. It testifies to the absolute need to make sense of the world in moral terms and of God's relation to it.

To avoid misunderstanding, it should be added that this kind of causal reasoning was part of the common theology of the ancient Near East which attributed evil to the anger of a deity resulting from sin, even inadvertent sin. According to this way of thinking, it was not necessary for the effect of sin to be felt at once. On the contrary, the interval between act and consequence could cover years or even generations. A prayer of Mursilis II, Hittite king of the fourteenth century BC, was occasioned by a plague which was ravaging the land; the cause of this was discovered, on consultation of an oracle, to be the violation of a treaty with the Egyptians in the previous reign.

This brought on the anger of Teshub, the Hittite storm god, whose name had been invoked in the treaty. Rather similar is David's consulting of an oracle to discover the cause of a three-year famine at the beginning of his reign. This turned out to be Saul's violation of his treaty oath with the Gibeonites several years earlier, and the matter was only resolved after seven of his descendants had been put to death (2 Sam. 21: 1-14).

The same principle is in evidence in the history of David's family to which we have alluded more than once in the previous chapters. The death of the anonymous child born of David's illicit union with Bathsheba is attributed directly to the anger of Yahweh: 'the thing that David had done displeased Yahweh . . . and Yahweh struck the child that Uriah's wife bore to David, and it became sick' (2 Sam. 11: 27; 12: 15). The ruinous fratricidal strife which broke out among his remaining sons is traced to the same source, as revealed to him in advance by Nathan the seer: 'the sword shall never depart from your house, because you have despised me, and have taken the wife of Uriah the Hittite to be your wife' (2 Sam. 12: 10). This principle of theological causality can be illustrated from several incidents in biblical narratives. In the so-called primeval history (Gen. 1-11) it is worked out with the help of mythological themes in the broader context of the history of the human family as a whole.

In the prophetic writings the link between sin and punishment — the latter in the form of political disaster — is the more prominent in that the prophets make extensive use of the political analogy of covenant with its associations of overlordship, binding obligations reinforced by curses, and the direct communication of the sovereign's will. If questioned, a prophet like Amos or Jeremiah might well have agreed that sin brings about its effect on the sinner by virtue of its own inner dynamic. This, however, would not be incompatible with the direct judicial intervention of God in the life of the individual and the state. The pattern can be seen in the condemnation of Saul by Samuel, presented as a model of prophetic opposition to the monarchy (1 Sam. 15; cf. 13: 7-15). Though Saul's decision to spare Agag seems positively meritorious to the modern reader, it was condemned by Samuel as a violation of the ban leading to divine rejection and consequent fall from power. Typically, the Chronicler, writing several centuries later, states the lesson explicitly:

> So Saul died for his unfaithfulness; he was unfaithful to Yahweh in that he did not keep the command of Yahweh, and also consulted a medium, seeking guidance, and did not seek guidance from Yahweh. Therefore Yahweh slew him, and turned the kingdom over to David the son of Jesse. (1 Chr. 10: 13-14).

Later still, Josephus will retell the story of Saul as a flawed hero in the manner of Greek tragedy, his final *peripateia* or change of fortune occurring when he conjured up Samuel's ghost (*Antiquities* 6: 45-378).

For the prophets, then, political disaster was the result of divine punishment incurred on account of sin, the more severe in the case of Israel because of the special relationship which bound her to Yahweh (e.g. Am. 3: 2, 14). Indeed this correlation between human act and divine reaction — whether described as rewarding and punishing, or remembering and forgetting, or in some other way — provided the prophets with the key to deciphering the course of history and projecting the future.

While much about the origins of the Deuteronomic programme is obscure, it would be widely accepted that it corresponds in some way to a movement of social and cultic reform which achieved full official acceptance during the reign of Josiah, the last great king of Judah (640-609 BC). It also provides us with the first clear evidence for the administration and interpretation of a law book by the scribal classes. While a more thorough discussion of this book must be postponed to Chapter 4, we should note for our present purpose that Yahweh is often represented in it as a teacher who disciplines his people by word of mouth (Deut. 4: 36) and through the vicissitudes of history (8: 5). Its trials in the wilderness are viewed as a necessary preparation for life in the land (8: 2, 16), and even false prophecy can serve as a kind of testing (13: 3). Deuteronomy abounds in the kind of moralizing and educational language which we associate with the sages. Exhortations to keep the law are routinely reinforced by motivation clauses of the kind we noted earlier in Proverbs: keep the law and you will live long in the land; neglect it and you will end up in exile (4: 1, 25-7, 40, etc.).

An identical perspective dominates the history of the kingdoms the final edition of which dates from the exilic period and the author or authors of which belonged to the Deuteronomic school. The pattern is established right from the beginning. Military success against the Canaanites depends on observance of the law (Jos. 1: 8). The history of Israel's heroic age preceding the monarchy is organized according to the same principle: the Israelites fell into apostasy thus provoking Yahweh to anger; this brought on military disaster which in its turn induced a change of heart; Yahweh sent a military leader to save them in response to their plea for assistance; after the death of the leader they lapsed once again into apostasy and the process was repeated (Judg. 2: 11-23 etc.). During the monarchy the political success of rulers and dynasties is contingent on their religious fidelity. The collapse of the Northern Kingdom results from the setting up of a separatist cult by Jeroboam and the sins of the Omrid dynasty (2 Kgs. 17: 21; cf. Mic. 6: 16). The fall of Jerusalem can be traced back to the apostasy of Manasseh who died more than half a century earlier (2 Kgs. 21: 10-15; 23: 26-7; 24: 3-4). From beginning to end the history is dominated by this law of moral causality which also serves to explain and justify the divine judgment which overtook the nation and its rulers.

Political disaster and religious crisis

In any society a religion, or its equivalent, provides a basic orientation and cohesive world view which is usually strong enough to survive the occasional inevitable discrepancy between theory and experience. Naturally, there will always be individuals whose experience will lead them to question, and sometimes even to reject, the account of reality offered by the religion. It is therefore not surprising that several psalms quote the wicked as, in effect, denying the existence of God, which means denying the possibility of divine intervention in their affairs:

> In the pride of his countenance the wicked does

not seek him;
all his thoughts are, 'There is no God',　(10: 4)

or, more simply:

The fool says in his heart, 'There is no God'
(14: 1; 53: 1)

Scepticism about the power, reality, or justice of God is also heard occasionally in the prophetic books; as, for example, when the people of Jerusalem say, 'Yahweh will not do good, nor will he do ill' (Zeph. 1: 12; cf. Ezek. 8: 12; 9: 9). To this we must add that the prospect of wickedness unrequited or, worse, rewarded with temporal prosperity, could present an almost insuperable obstacle to the faith of those who remained faithful. So we hear, again in the psalms, laments that God has forgotten, that he has hidden his face, that perhaps he is not aware of what is going on (e.g. Ps. 10: 11; 73: 11; 125: 3). The sages also attest that the experience of adversity can lead a person to the breaking point. As one proverb puts it:

When a man's folly brings his way to ruin,
his heart rages against Yahweh.　(Prov. 19: 3)

At some time during the Persian period people were complaining that 'everyone who does evil is good in the sight of Yahweh', leading to the question, 'where is the God of justice?' (Mal. 2: 17). Clearly, then, a conflict between the theory of moral causality and experience could easily lead to raising questions about the ethical character of God as sustainer of the moral order.

The shortest, and certainly the most obscure section of Proverbs, attributed to a certain Agur ben-Yakeh (Prov. 30: 1-6), testifies to the emergence of the same crisis of faith among the sages themselves. The textual obscurity of this short passage, reflected in the widely differing English versions, may well be the result of a deliberate attempt to conceal sentiments too much at odds with orthodox beliefs. Any interpretation, therefore, is bound to be hypothetical. A possible reconstruction of the sage's opening words would run as follows:

There is no god, there is no god, and I am weary . . .

> For I am more beast than man,
> I do not possess human knowledge,
> I have not learned wisdom
> to have knowledge of the Most High.

This affirmation, and the rhetorical questions which follow, would seem to be addressed ironically to the sceptic's 'learned colleagues' who seem to know everything about God that is to be known. The approach is therefore not essentially different from that of Qoheleth, to be discussed shortly, though the latter affirms the reality of God while denying that we can know anything about his nature and operations. A final comment (Prov. 30: 5-6) states that God has made himself known through his word and discourages the kind of theological speculation which, in the case of Agur, ended in frustration and negation.

This enigmatic text is one of the later components of Proverbs, perhaps from the late Persian or early Hellenistic period. About the same time the Chronicler was writing his version of the history from David to Ezra and Nehemiah (1 and 2 Chronicles, Ezra, Nehemiah). Like his principal source, the Deuteronomic History, the author sees the link between act and consequence as one of the keys for understanding the course of events and, at times, formulates it quite explicitly. In order to explain how Manasseh, a reprobate according to his source, could have reigned so long, he adds an account of how he repented and even has him carrying out religious reforms in the capital (2 Chr. 33: 10-17). Josiah, on the other hand, was a good king who nevertheless died young. The Chronicler, therefore, adds a notice to the effect that he wilfully disregarded a divine oracle communicated through the Egyptian king (2 Chr. 35: 21-2). This may serve to show that quite different points of view could be proposed during roughly the same period of time, and therefore will remind us that what is known as 'the religion of Israel' must be understood to take in quite different and even conflicting perspectives and opinions.

The Chronicler's determination to bring events into line with theological doctrine shows the urgency of the problem posed by the historical experience of Israel. With the destruction of Jerusalem by the Babylonians in 586 BC the problem for many became insoluble. Understandably, it has left a deep imprint on the writings which have survived from that time.

Written shortly after the tragic death of Josiah in 609, Habakkuk opens with an agonizing appeal for divine justice to be manifest:

> Yahweh, how long shall I cry for help,
>   and thou wilt not hear?
> Or cry to thee, 'Violence!'
>   and thou wilt not save?   (1: 2)

The note of agony is also heard in certain psalm-like passages in Jeremiah (e.g. 12: 1-4) and in hymns which, if they do not come from that time, reflect such a situation of total destitution (e.g. Pss. 44; 74; 79). A lament, possibly composed shortly after the fall of Jerusalem, poses the issue more sharply:

> Our fathers sinned, and are no more;
>   and we bear their iniquities.   (Lam. 5: 7)

It also found expression in a proverb which circulated at that time: 'the fathers have eaten sour grapes and the children's teeth are set on edge' (Jer. 31: 29-30; Ezek. 18: 2). The issue, then, was the fate of the innocent caught in the destructive flow of events which people had been taught to think were under the control of a powerful and just God. Given traditional religious beliefs, the massive disasters of the early sixth century BC could only mean that either Yahweh was powerless to prevent them happening or that he had decided to punish his people in a manner totally out of proportion to their wrongdoing. Hence the accusation of injustice levelled against God — 'the way of Yahweh is not just' (Ezek. 18: 25, 29; 33: 17, 20).

One of those most concerned to counter this charge was Ezekiel, a prophet deported to Babylon shortly before the fall of Jerusalem. He argued that each generation, indeed each individual, stood on its own in the matter of moral responsibility and the imputation of guilt. Using the traditional form of casuistic law, he presented the test case of a family through three generations: a good man who has an evil son who, in his turn, has a son who does not follow his bad example. The conclusion: there is no carry-over from one generation to the next by virtue of the way divine justice is administered, and the point is reinforced by emphasizing the possibility of conversion (Ezek. 18: 5-29; cf. 33: 10-20). Elsewhere Ezekiel applied the same principle to the destruction of Jerusalem. In a vision dated five years before that event took place, he recorded that the righteous few were marked with a cross which guaranteed their survival (9: 1-11).

Since it was natural to conceive of divine justice as in some way analogous with judicial procedures in force in the society, Ezekiel's argument can be read simply as an acknowledgement that the justice of God must, at the least, come up to the best standards according to which human justice is administered. In the Deuteronomic law book the principle of corporate liability continued in force only in the exceptional cases of apostasy and homicide (Deut. 13: 12-18; 21: 1-9). In all other cases the emphasis was firmly on the responsibility of the individual:

> The fathers shall not be put to death for the children, nor shall the children be put to death for the fathers; everyone shall be put to death for his own sin. (24: 16)

This is, of course, rather different from the old cultic confession in which Yahweh is said to visit the iniquity of the fathers upon the children to the third and fourth generation (Ex. 34: 7; Num. 14: 18). An interesting case of development can be seen in the decalogue which takes up this formula and adds the phrase 'of those who hate me' (Ex. 20: 5; Deut. 5: 9). We must suppose that the purpose of this addition is to make it clear that, if there is solidarity in guilt between the generations, it is because the children imitate the sins of their parents and not by virtue of the way God administers justice. Ezekiel clearly expresses the same point of view, taking up and developing a more mature and reflective approach to the moral responsibility of the individual.

If political disaster focussed attention on the effect of the guilty on the fate of the innocent, it also forced people to reflect on the other side of the issue. In other words, given the existence of some righteous people in the doomed city, a possibility acknowledged by Ezekiel, the question arises whether they could not have influenced

God to spare the city at the cost of leaving the unrighteous majority unpunished. Ezekiel himself ruled out this possibility in one of his typical case histories. If a land was devastated by war, pestilence, and other disasters, and there lived in it those models of righteousness, Noah, Daniel, and Job, they would save no one, not even their sons and daughters, but only themselves (14: 12–23). It seems that at this point Ezekiel is dependent on Jeremiah's account of a famine during which it was revealed to him that God would not listen to the prayers of a sinful people, not even if Moses and Samuel, those masters of intercessory prayer, stood before him (Jer. 14: 1 – 15: 4). This seems to reflect the conviction, shared by many, that the destruction of the city was due in large measure to the failure of prophetic intercession (Jer. 7: 16; 11: 14; Ezek. 9: 8–10).

The question whether the righteous can influence the fate of the guilty is answered in a quite different way in the dialogue between Abraham and God over the fate of Sodom (Gen. 18: 22–33). God had decided to destroy the city on account of its moral depravity, thus raising the same issue of discriminating between the good and the wicked. Abraham makes the point with great force: 'Far be it from thee to do such a thing, to slay the innocent with the guilty. Far be it from thee! Shall not the judge of all the earth give right judgment?' But there is also the question whether a certain critical mass of righteous people can save the city. As Abraham's dramatic intercession gets the minimum required number down to ten, it emerges that such a critical mass does not exist. Yet ten would have sufficed, and so the possibility is here affirmed whereas in Ezekiel it is denied – another example of divergent solutions and points of view within the biblical canon. This affirmation will be very important in later religious developments in Judaism and Christianity. It has connections with the prophetic Servant of Second Isaiah who will 'make many to be accounted righteous' (Isa. 53: 11). Still later it will re-emerge in the belief, expounded in the midrash, that at any time in history there are thirty-six hidden saints whose righteousness sustains the world – a theme which underlies André Schwarz-Bart's famous novel, *The Last of the Just*.

In view of the peculiar character of this passage, quite unlike any other in Genesis, together with the fact that Jerusalem is sometimes referred to in prophetic diatribe as Sodom (e.g. Isa. 1: 9-10; 3: 9; Jer. 23: 14), it may be read as a later addition to the Sodom narrative which has in mind the destruction of Jerusalem and the theological questions to which that momentous event gave rise. The central issue was the fate of the righteous in a world − or city − over which the God of Israel claimed jurisdiction. We must now see how this issue was dealt with in a much longer composition, though one in other respects quite similar, from the post-exilic period.

Job

The protagonist of this book is one of the three righteous men living in a devastated land who will not be able to save anyone but themselves by their righteousness (Ezek. 14: 12-20). The narrative setting is the long ago time of the ancestors among the people of the east (1: 3 cf. Gen. 29: 1), when wealth was measured by numerous servants and livestock, and longevity was the rule. The place is the land of Uz (1: 1), also known to the ancestors (Gen. 22: 21). Like Abraham, Job is righteous, a servant of God (1: 8 cf. Gen. 26: 24), one who intercedes for others (42: 8-9 cf. Gen. 20: 7), who is tested by God and survives with his faith intact.

Like the Job of Ezek. 14: 12-20 the protagonist, though righteous, cannot save even his children, much less the many others afflicted by the disasters which struck the land of Uz. He is therefore left to try to make sense of what had happened and to struggle for faith in a God who, though judge of all the earth, appeared to destroy the innocent along with the guilty (9: 22-4 cf. Gen. 18: 25). He is also like Abraham in daring, though but dust and ashes (42: 6 cf. Gen. 18: 27), to demand that God live up to the best standards according to which human justice is administered.

Since some of the most difficult problems in the interpretation of the book arise out of its structure, it may be useful to lay this out at once:

Narrative prologue: alternating scenes on earth and in heaven (1-2)
Job's monologue (3)

Debate between Job and the 'friends': Eliphaz, Zophar, Bildad
(4-27)
First series (4-14)
Second series (15-21)
Third series (22-7)
Poem on inaccessible wisdom (28)
Job's oath of clearance and summons to God to appear (29-31)
Elihu's contribution (32-7)
God answers Job who submits (38: 1 – 40: 5; 40: 6 – 42: 6)
Narrative epilogue: Job restored to good estate (42: 7-17).

It will be seen that a narrative framework encloses a debate between Job and four sages ending in a direct appeal by Job to God
that he appear and state his case. After the divine response to this
appeal Job submits and the matter is ended. Certain indications
of editorial activity which disturb the logical order may be noted.
The third series in the debate is confused, and the confusion may be
explained in part on the assumption that Zophar's contribution has
been transferred, accidentally or deliberately, to Job. The poem on
wisdom (28), one of the most powerful in the Hebrew Bible, was
originally an independent composition and is here attributed, not
entirely appropriately, to Job. (It will be discussed at greater length
in the last chapter of this book.) Elihu's lengthy harangue is clearly
intrusive and quite unexpected after the notice that the words of
Job are ended (31: 40). That it was added after the work was
essentially complete is suggested by the allusions in it to God's
answer to Job, quite apart from the fact that only three respondents
had been introduced and are to re-appear in the epilogue. Its insertion delays the sequel to Job's summons, which is of course the
appearance and reply of God. It seems, finally, that the book has
preserved two accounts of God's answer and Job's reaction to his
appearance.

It has long been noted that the narrative framework does not
make a perfect fit with the body of the work. At the most obvious
level, the long-suffering Job of the prologue undergoes a startling
transformation once he begins to soliloquize and reply to his 'friends'.
So also the latter, who keep silent and sympathetic vigil at the outset,

progressively reveal themselves to be far from friendly as the debate gathers momentum. The God of the narrative is Yahweh, Israel's own God, whereas the God who is spoken of and who speaks in the body of the work bears the more generic names, common to Semitic antiquity, of El, Eloah, and Shaddai. More importantly, the narrative appears to affirm what it is the purpose of the debate to call into question, i.e., that innocence is always vindicated and guilt always punished. In the course of the debate Job is taken to task by God for his intemperate speech, while in the prose epilogue the 'friends' are castigated for not having spoken well of God. There is also the curious fact that the Satan, who appears at the beginning as the occasion of Job's atrocious suffering, is not heard of again.

It is for these reasons that many commentators have been led to the conclusion that the debate, the purpose of which is to provide a new solution to the problem of undeserved suffering and the divine governance of the world, has been spliced into an old folktale which, in effect, re-affirms the traditional teaching of the sages on these issues. One problem with this view is, of course, the assumption that the final editor did not notice the discrepancy which is so obvious to the modern reader. One would also have thought that this point could have been made more clearly by simply telling the story of a just man who, like Abraham, is tested by God, comes through with flying colours, and is eventually restored to good fortune. What calls for an explanation is precisely the juxtaposition of narrative and debate or, in other words, the final shape of the work irrespective of whatever editorial stages led up to it. And since in its final form it begins and ends in narrative it must be interpreted as a narrative work, which means that we must ask what happens to the hero — and to others — in the course of it.

Beginning with the prologue which, with the epilogue, is in prose, Job is presented as a righteous man blessed with a large family and many possessions. His children were in the habit of celebrating the festivals in each others' houses, on which occasions Job would offer sacrifices to make amends for any secret sins which they might commit. Meanwhile, a different kind of assembly was taking place in heaven. The scenario here has clear analogies with other heavenly scenes in the Hebrew Bible, including the prophetic visions of Isaiah

(6: 1-13) and Micaiah (1 Kgs. 22: 19-23). Summoned by king Ahab to give a favourable oracle before battle, Micaiah reported a vision in which Yahweh asked for a volunteer among the attendants at his court to go and deceive the king so that he should die in battle. One of these, referred to simply as the Spirit, offered to discharge the task by being a lying spirit in the mouth of the prophets. The post-exilic prophet Zechariah also reported a vision in which Joshua the high priest was indicted unsuccessfully by the Satan standing at his right hand (Zech. 3: 1-5). This scenario of the divine court seems to have been borrowed from Canaanite mythology in which El, supreme god of the pantheon, is surrounded by lesser deities. The Satan, who is not, of course, the familiar figure of Christian imagination and art, appears as one of the attendants of the divine court in the act of making his report. As the name ('adversary' in Hebrew) suggests, his function is that of checking and testing the loyalty of Yahweh's subjects. He is a kind of *agent provocateur*, perhaps corresponding to the Persian functionary known as 'the eyes and ears of the king' whose task was to go around the provinces checking on local officials.

So, on the subject of Job, the Satan suggests that his piety is interested; in effect, a function of his prosperity. This leads to a kind of wager in which the Satan is permitted to deprive him of everything to see if he would curse God and, by so doing, sever relations with him. The string of disasters which follows, which affects others in the land of Uz besides Job, is represented as directly flowing from this conversation in heaven about which Job is, of course, ignorant. Yet Job did not sin by cursing God, not even when afflicted with a particularly atrocious form of skin disease.

The purpose of this prologue is not just to tell a story but to pose a problem. The suffering of the innocent is indeed attributable to God, being permitted as a test of integrity. The alternatives for the one subjected to this test are to accept it without question or to curse God, and to curse God means to attribute evil intent to him, to charge him with wrongdoing (1: 22). The manner of the testing raises, and is intended to raise, serious questions about the ethical character of God, questions which it is the purpose of the debate to explore. In this sense, at least, the prologue and the debate clearly belong together.

The opening soliloquy introduces a rather different Job who curses the night of his conception and the day of his birth, and voices his despair in dark images of stillbirth and death. To judge by their names, the debaters are Arabic sages testifying, together with the Arabs Agur and Lemuel of Proverbs, to the reputation for wisdom enjoyed by Edomites and Arabs. They are not intended to be straw men, mechanically reproducing arguments for Job to refute. On the contrary, they represent the best thinking available in the schools on the issue under discussion. Eliphaz opens the debate courteously, advancing the orthodox argument that innocence is always rewarded sooner or later, and adding the further lesson, for which the authority of a personal revelation is adduced, that no mortal is pure or wise enough to question God's dealings (4: 12-21). On this basis he tactfully suggests that Job examine his conscience, since only by confessing sin can the rationale of suffering and evil be maintained.

The second speaker, Bildad, proceeds on a somewhat more acrimonious note, explaining the death of Job's children on the grounds that God had allowed their (presumably secret) sins to catch up with them (8: 4). As for Job himself, he should consult the accumulated wisdom of the past which testifies that innocence is always vindicated, and that therefore his sufferings will come to an end if he is really as blameless as he claims to be. The third, Zophar, is the least accommodating of the three, accusing Job of wilful ignorance and stupidity in not acknowledging the infinite distance between God and humanity. He therefore also urges him to confess as a means of bringing his suffering to an end.

In his replies, Job expresses his hatred of life and longing for death, not because of his sufferings in themselves, but because God has, inexplicably, become his enemy. And here it is important to note that he desires death not because he hopes that injustice will be righted in a life after death, but only to put an end to the conscious-ness of pain (significantly, he never contemplates suicide). Life after death is, in fact, subsequently ruled out (see 7: 9-10). It is ironic that the only passage in the book likely to be familiar to the general reader — owing to the popularity of Handel's *Messiah* — is widely interpreted as an affirmation of the hope for immortality or resurrection:

> For I know that my Redeemer lives,
>   and at last he will stand upon the earth;
> and after my skin has been thus destroyed,
>   then from my flesh I shall see God.   (19: 25-26)

As it stands, the meaning is far from clear, and the reason is that the passage is textually corrupt, perhaps owing to its controversial nature. The context suggests that Job is expressing the desire that his case be recorded indelibly in writing in the hope of an at least post-humous vindication when the decisive witness of his innocence, to whom he despairingly appeals throughout the book (9: 32-3; 16: 19-21; 33: 23-4), will take his stand in court. In any case, as we have just seen, the finality of death is clearly affirmed by Job at other points of the debate (see also 10: 20-2; 14: 7-12).

The literary ability which is one of the characteristics of Israel's sages is abundantly in evidence in this first series of arguments and counter-arguments. So, for example, the author makes use of familiar hymn forms, putting psalms of individual lamentation into Job's mouth (e.g. 7: 1-11) while his opponents quote psalms of trust and confidence at him (e.g. 5: 17-27). Proverbs are also traded back and forth − not surprisingly, since it is a contest of sages − and there are other literary devices in use in the schools such as the rhetorical question (e.g. 6: 5-6). But most noteworthy is the use of forensic terminology, the language of the courtroom, especially in Job's answer to Bildad (9-10). He speaks of the impossibility of a fair trial when God is both accuser and judge, of issuing, or responding to, a summons to appear in court, of arguing his case with the assistance of a counsel for the defence, and so on. It seems that the author has chosen this forensic model deliberately as a means of presenting the case for both parties, God and Job. And since the same kind of legal language is used elsewhere in the Hebrew Bible in speaking of the covenant between God and the people (e.g., in the prophetic indictment of Israel for covenant infidelity), the likelihood is increased that the book deals with the crisis not just of an individual but of the nation. We have seen how the disasters of the early sixth century BC gave rise to the gravest theological problems and called into question the justice of God and his fidelity to the covenant made with the ancestors.

Eliphaz opened the second round of the debate by raising the question of authority, a matter of great importance for the sages. One could appeal to ancient tradition or, with the prophets, to personal revelation. In neither respect did Job qualify, since he was not the first man nor had he been admitted to the secret conclave of God (15: 7-8). Indeed, he was not even all that old that he should speak with such assurance (15: 10). By now, however, it is apparent that Job is no longer interested in refuting the arguments of his interlocutors; it is a matter between himself and God alone. And so he takes his life in his hands since he has nothing to lose, and does not hold back in accusing God of indifference to the human condition, of massively undermining human hope, even of murder;

> It is all one; therefore I say,
>> he destroys both the blameless and the wicked.
> When disaster brings sudden death,
>> he mocks at the calamity of the innocent.
> The earth is given into the hands of the wicked;
>> he covers the faces of its judges −
>> if it is not he, who then is it?   (9: 22-4)

> The waters wear away the stones . . .
>> so thou destroyest the hope of man.   (14: 19)

> O earth, cover not my blood,
>> and let my cry find no resting place!.   (16: 18)

In the third and last series the contrasting positions are stated in their most extreme and stark form, so much so that the disjointed sequence of speakers and ideas is probably due to later attempts to mitigate the violence of the accusations levelled against the God of traditional religion. As it is, Job conjures up a terrible vision of a world where moral chaos rules supreme, in which power is triumphant and the poor trampled into the ground, over which presides a God who chooses not to intervene. His accusation may be translated as follows:

> From the city the dying groan,
> the throat of the wounded cries,
> yet God sees nothing amiss.   (24: 12)

In a different context all of this would be nothing more nor less than blasphemy; but with Job it arises, paradoxically, from his refusal to break off relations with God, to take his wife's advice to 'curse God and die'. Since he speaks in the assurance that 'a godless man shall not come before him' (13: 16), it is, in effect, a violent form of prayer uttered *in extremis*.

The poem on wisdom (chapter 28), which will be discussed at length in Chapter 6 (pp. 132-6), is ascribed to Job in the present state of the text (27: 1). Since, however, the passage immediately preceding (27: 13-23) is a traditional description of how the wicked man comes to a bad end, the order has certainly been disturbed. It would, in addition, be rather surprising to find Job at this point equating wisdom with 'the fear of Yahweh' (28: 28). Job's final discourse (29-31) contrasts earlier days, when God was his friend, with present miseries in the manner of those psalms of lamentation which open with a recital of past divine favours, go on to describe present misfortunes, and end with an appeal to God to remember and make his presence felt (e.g. Ps. 89). The climax of his peroration, and of the debate as a whole, is the oath of clearance couched in the form of confession of innocence – not unlike the Egyptian Books of the Dead – and sealed with self-imposed curses. At this point the forensic metaphor is quite explicit. In Israelite legal practice the taking of the oath of clearance by an accused party, even in capital cases, resulted in the accusation being dropped and the accused being left to his own devices. The sages therefore are at last silenced and Job summons God to appear and state his case (31: 35-7). He does appear, but not until Elihu, the angry young man of the poem, has had his say.

Since the contribution of Elihu comes from a later hand, we may suppose that it was added out of dissatisfaction with the debate, or at least because it was thought something essential had been omitted. It is even possible that these speeches were added to a book which ended with the colophon, 'the words of Job are ended' (31: 40), and that therefore they were meant to be a final judgment on the debate. And in fact Elihu does find both parties deficient in that God, by his nature, is immeasurably superior to both the rationalizations of the sages and the importunate demands of Job. He certainly stresses the absolute freedom of God who cannot be questioned and who makes himself known on his own terms and in his own ways (e.g. 33: 12-18; 35: 6-7). Suffering is a divine discipline, and the appropriate response is an attitude of humble acceptance (33: 19-28). These are not unimportant considerations, and highlight once again the variety and depth of reflection on theological issues among the scribes of the Second Temple period.

God finally answered Job's summons, but not in the way Job intended or anticipated. The voice from the whirlwind is patterned on prophetic descriptions of the theophany:

> You will be visited by Yahweh of hosts
>   with thunder and with earthquake and with great noise,
>   with whirlwind and tempest, and the flame of a devouring
>   fire. (Is. 29: 6)

The actual message, however, reflects the sages' learned preoccupation with the wonders of nature; witness the detailed descriptions of ostrich (39: 13-18), horse (39: 19-25), hawk (29: 26-30), hippopotamus (40: 15-24), and crocodile (41: 1-34). But the important point is that the God who reveals himself to Job is not a God who can be circumscribed by learned debate in the schools, or about whom calculations can be made, or with whom contractual arrangements can be drawn up. In this respect the author reflects the shift towards a more transcendental and universalist understanding of Yahweh to which the national disasters of the sixth century certainly contributed. In that sense, both Job and his learned colleagues stand under judgment.

For many readers, however, there will still be the scandal that God does not address himself to Job's question or, what is even worse, answers the question of justice with a display of power which simply confirms the existence of the problem. This may mean that there is simply no answer to the problem so posed, or that faith must not be contingent on receiving a divine assurance that it will all turn out well in the end. And, when all is said and done, God does finally show that he is present. In this respect, comparison with Ps. 73, a didactic rather than cultic composition, may be useful. The poet begins with the same problem as Job, that of the triumph of evil in a world believed to be under the governance of a just God. There is no theoretical solution, but none is needed once the perplexed questioner enters the sanctuary, experiences the reality of the divine presence and, like Job, makes his confession:

> When my soul was embittered,
>> when I was pricked in heart,
> I was stupid and ignorant,
>> I was like a beast toward thee.
> Nevertheless I am continually with thee;
>> thou dost hold my right hand . . .   (Ps. 73: 21–3)

> I had heard of thee by the hearing of the ear,
>> but now my eye sees thee;
> therefore I despise myself,
>> and repent in dust and ashes.   (Job 42: 5–6)

To come back, finally, to the narrative character of the work: something happens to Job, something within his own painful experience which changes everything. The book might well have ended here, with his confession and submission (42: 6). Indeed, the fragmentary targum or paraphrase of Job from the eleventh cave at Qumran (11QtgJob), which ends at 42: 11, shows that there was some hesitation as to where the book should end as late as the second century BC when the targum was written. The epilogue, at any rate, does no more than suggest that, if the traditional teaching on retribution continues in force, it must be in a form which allows faith to be independent of self-interest and which takes account of the intractable and painful data of experience.

Qoheleth

The problem with which the author of Job struggled was obviously not confined to one place or one moment of time, however critical.

A Sumerian scribal composition from the first half of the second millennium BC, translated under the title of 'The Sumerian Job' or 'Man and His God', speaks of an innocent young man who, like Job, is afflicted with sickness. Calumniated on this account by his associates, who attribute his condition to a god's anger brought about by sin, he prays earnestly and confesses his sins with the result that his affliction is turned into joy. Unlike Job, however, he does not question divine justice. We come upon a similar situation in a Babylonian psalm entitled 'I will praise the lord of wisdom' (*ludlul bel nemeqi*). As a result of sickness, the worshipper has been slandered and ostracized. He nevertheless continues in his devotion to Marduk, whose ways are acknowledged to be inscrutable, and eventually receives assurance in a dream of a happy outcome.

A more speculative and didactic composition from a somewhat later time, translated under the title 'The Babylonian Theodicy', presents a dialogue between an innocent sufferer and a friendly sage. Like Job, the former contrasts his misfortune with the prosperity of the wicked, is accused of impiety for his pains, and is assured that the wicked will get their desserts sooner or later. The proper response to suffering is piety towards the gods, even while admitting that the world created by them is flawed.

Strictly speaking, this last is the only composition from the ancient Near East which deals with the problem of divine justice and is therefore comparable to the biblical Job. There are writings which describe a reversal of fortune brought about by divine intervention in the manner of the Job epilogue. The Keret epic from Bronze Age Ugarit, for example, tells of a king who lost his entire family and eventually gained another with the help of the gods. What is lacking, however, is the essential element of focussing on the action and character of deity as problematic.

Quite different is the so-called 'Dialogue of Pessimism', a Mesopotamian text from the first millennium BC, where the starting point is not suffering and deprivation but ennui. A lord makes a series of proposals to do certain things such as dining, going for a ride in the country, and so on, and his servant urges him to do so, providing what appear to be excellent reasons; whereupon the lord changes his mind and the servant comes up with even stronger reasons for not doing them. The conversation goes somewhat as follows:

> 'Servant, listen to me.' 'Yes, master, yes.' 'I am going to make love to a woman.' 'So make love, master, make love. The man who makes love to a woman forgets sorrow and worry.' 'No, servant, I will not make love to a woman.' 'Do not make love, master, do not make love. A woman is a pitfall, a hole, a ditch, a woman is a sharp iron dagger that slits a man's throat.'

Not without a certain cynical humour, the dialogue makes short shrift of the 'consolations of religion' and proceeds to its terminus in the decision to commit suicide. Comparisons are often made between this text and the biblical Ecclesiastes (Qoheleth) but, as we shall now see, the similarity is more apparent than real.

Qoheleth occurs as a personal name in the title of the book (1: 1), but in the postscript (12: 8) and the body of the work (7: 27) it stands for an office or function. The Old Greek translation (Septuagint) and the Vulgate, followed by RSV, interpret this as an ecclesiastical office (*ecclesiastes*, preacher), but even a rapid glance at the book reveals that there is little ecclesiastical about its author. The Hebrew term should therefore be rendered 'teacher' or perhaps 'orator'. The attribution to Solomon, made in the title but sustained only in the first part of the work (1: 12 – 2: 26), is of course a literary fiction. Its significance is that it places the work within the established sapiential tradition deriving from Solomon. It also allowed the author to direct a radical criticism at the optimism, pragmatism and self-assurance of that tradition from within.

Taking on the mantle of the wisest of kings also, in all probability, suggested the form of the work, which is that of a royal testament featuring personal reminiscence. A familiar type of instruction in ancient Egypt, it would have seemed appropriate during the epoch of Ptolemaic rule – the third century BC – when the book was probably written. For the Ptolemies, whose court was in Alexandria, saw themselves as successors of the pharaohs and promoted a revival of pharaonic style both in life and in letters.

Whatever the original form of the work, a later scribe put it in the more familiar category of 'sayings of the sages' (12: 9-11 cf. Prov. 1: 6; 22: 17, 23):

> Besides being wise, the Preacher also taught the people knowledge, weighing and studying and arranging proverbs with great care. The Preacher sought to find pleasing words, and uprightly he wrote words of truth. The sayings of the wise are like goads, and like nails firmly fixed are the collected sayings which are given by one Shepherd.

This editorial postscript is clearly an *apologia* for the author's work which must have been controversial. It identifies him as a sage and teacher who worked with proverbs — as the book in fact demonstrates — and found the right language to make his students think for themselves. It is followed by a final note, probably from a different hand:

> My son, beware of anything beyond these. Of making many books there is no end, and much study is a weariness of the flesh. The end of the matter; all has been heard. Fear God, and keep his commandments; for this is the whole duty of man. For God will bring every deed into judgment, with every secret thing, whether good or evil.

Here we have a warning against speculative writings over and above those which had already won official approval, including Ecclesiastes. It may therefore be read as indicating a mature stage in the formation of the canonical books. This editor's summary of the book — to fear God and keep his commandments in the light of divine judgment — presupposes the insertion of more orthodox sentiments at various points in it (e.g. 3: 17; 7: 18; 8: 12-13; 11: 9). It is an interesting interpretation and explains at once why Ecclesiastes won acceptance into the scriptural canon. Whether the author himself would have agreed with it as an adequate summary of his own thinking is another matter.

Though Ecclesiastes has generally been thought to lack any firm structure, the first part at least (1: 3 — 2: 26) presents a consistent and well-arranged argument. After the tone is set with a refrain which sounds like a tolling bell throughout the work — 'emptiness,

emptiness, all is empty' (NEB) — Qoheleth argues that both human history and the phenomena of nature suggest an endless, predetermined cyclical process which excludes novelty and deprives human effort of ultimate significance. This conclusion is confirmed by personal experience; and here the author speaks as Solomon. The search for pleasure and wisdom, the amassing of wealth, the doing of great deeds — all of these end in frustration since they end in death and, in due time, oblivion. The first and natural reaction is despair — hatred of life and self-hatred — which however, unlike the Mesopotamian text, does not end in suicide. On the contrary, Qoheleth leads us from the certainty of death to the positive acceptance of life and whatever limited satisfactions it has to offer:

> There is nothing better for a man than that he should eat and drink, and find enjoyment in his toil. This also, I saw, is from the hand of God. (2: 24)

We find here, right at the beginning, a cardinal point in the teaching of this exceptional thinker. Death undermines the structures of meaning by which the wisdom tradition makes sense of life. It also frustrates the practical means by which it sought to bring human action under the control of rationality. More than any other event, it lies outside human control and defies explanation. For Qoheleth, it is, quite simply, *fate* (2: 14-15; 3: 19; 9: 2-3), an idea found nowhere else in the Hebrew Bible and, in fact, foreign to biblical thought. (Isa. 65: 11 refers to Gad and Meni, gods of fortune, but their cult is condemned). Yet, paradoxically, wherever this conclusion is reached, it is followed at once by the affirmation of life, with all its limitations, as the *portion* of humankind under the inscrutable dispensation of God (3: 22; 5: 18; 9: 9). The practical and ethical corollary is that only when death is accepted without the illusions which the fear of death so easily generates can one really begin to accept life as a gift.

It is extremely important to distinguish Qoheleth's point of view from the kind of despairing hedonism which the thought of the finality of death often inspires. The contrast will be apparent in the words which the author of The Wisdom of Solomon (to be discussed in Chapter 6) puts in the mouth of the Jew who has abandoned his traditional religion under the allure of popular Epicurean philosophy:

> 'Short and sorrowful is our life,
> and there is no remedy when a man comes to his end,
> and no one has been known to return from Hades.
> Because we were born by mere chance,
> and hereafter we shall be as though we had never
>   been . . .
> For our allotted time is the passing of a shadow,
> and there is no return from our death,
> because it is sealed up and no one turns back.
> Come, therefore, let us enjoy the good things
>   that exist,
> and make use of the creation to the full, as in
>   youth.
> Let us take our fill of costly wine and perfumes,
> and let no flower of spring pass by us.
> Let us crown ourselves with rosebuds before they
>   wither.
> Let none of us fail to share in our revelry,
> everywhere let us leave signs of enjoyment,
> because this is our portion, and this is our lot.'
>
>   (Wisd. 2: 1–9)

While it is entirely possible that Qoheleth was familiar with Epicurean philosophy — of which, incidentally, this quotation is something of a caricature — his philosophy of death does not derive from this source. If there is any analogy with philosophical views of late antiquity, it would be with the Stoic distinction between the things which are and are not within our control, as expounded, for example, in the *Moral Discourses* of Epictetus. Of all things death is least under our control, and to accept this situation is to free the mind from a major source of crippling anxiety. But whatever possible analogies may be proposed, it seems that Qoheleth is offering a positive answer to the numbing question which death poses to any reflective person.

The didactic poem which follows this first section (3: 1–15) develops further the author's philosophical view of time in relation to the divine dispensation. There is an appropriate time for each human act − an important consideration since it is part of wisdom to do everything at the proper time. Each of these moments is measured on the continuum of God's time (translated 'eternity' in RSV, 3: 11). The human mind can arrive at the point of acknowledging that this is so, but this knowledge does not translate into the ability to act appropriately, to exercise control over one's life. God has predetermined everything in advance; nothing can be changed; the circle is closed (3: 14-15). Time is God's time, but we do not have the key to crack the code. This is a major theme of Qoheleth which recurs throughout the work. Thus, in keeping with his method of subjecting traditional gnomic wisdom to criticism, he quotes a proverb:

> What is crooked cannot be made straight,
> and what is lacking cannot be numbered. (1: 15)

and restates it, at a later point, with astonishing theological candour:

> Consider the work of God;
> who can make straight what he has made crooked?
> (7: 13)

This work of God, he goes on to say, is the fortuitous incidence of good and evil fortune to which experience attests; and it happens so that we may never know what the future holds (3: 14, cf. 8: 6-7). The sages claim to be able to fathom what goes on on earth, to make sense of it as God's work, but they are mistaken (8: 17). If the sages were right, things would work out as they predict, but it does not happen that way. Humankind is the creature of chance, at the mercy of circumstances beyond its control (9: 11-12).

The inescapable consequence of this position is that the link between act and consequence, and therefore the idea of divine retribution, is called into question. This leads quite logically to the issue of unrequited evil and injustice which Qoheleth goes on to address (3: 16 − 4: 3). As always, he begins with experience: 'Moreover I saw under the sun that in the place of justice, even there was wickedness, and in the place of righteousness, even there was wickedness' (3: 16). He then, typically, quotes an orthodox proverb to the effect that in due time the scandal of triumphant injustice will be righted by God (3: 17). But then, he continues, our actual experience of evil could as well demonstrate that humankind is on the same level as the animals. Both, after all, are subject to the same fate, since ideas about astral immortality current in the contemporary world are pure speculation: 'Who knows whether the spirit of man goes upward and the spirit of the beast goes down to the earth?' (3: 21). Put aside such speculation, he concludes, and get on with the job of living.

Unlike the prophets, Qoheleth does not propose to do anything about injustice in the world. It is one of those things outside our control that we must learn to live with — an attitude probably shared by many whose lives were controlled by the massive bureaucratic machine of the Ptolemaic monarchy (cf. 5: 8–20; 8: 2–9). He does, however, offer some penetrating reflections on the contemporary rat race (4: 4–16). With the help of proverbs (vss. 5, 6, 9–13) he notes how rivalry, competition, keeping up with others, lead to isolation and alienation. People never stop to ask: why am I doing all this? His conclusion: that human companionship, genuine society, is the only antidote to the inevitable miseries and vexations of life.

There can be no doubt that for Qoheleth the fundamental issue is religious; that is to say, it has to do with what we can know about God and what consequences follow from that knowledge. His relationship to the traditional and ancestral religion is tenuous to say the least, and his attitude to the external expressions of that religion — animal sacrifice, prayer, vows, etc. — is critical and detached:

Guard your steps when you go to the house of God; to draw near to listen is better than to offer the sacrifice of fools; for they do not know that they are doing evil. Be not rash with your mouth, nor let your heart be hasty to utter a word before God, for God is in heaven, and you upon earth; therefore let your words be few . . . When you vow a vow to God, do not delay paying it; for he has no pleasure in fools. Pay what you vow. It is better that you should not vow than that you should vow and not pay.
(5: 1–5)

God is transcendent and unknowable. Everything is under his control, but whether in love or hate we do not know (9: 1); nor does he vouchsafe to satisfy the human demand for justice. Yet the practical outcome is not denial or rejection of God but an attitude of fear and reverence (3: 14; 5: 7; 7: 18), together with a positive ethic of grateful acceptance of life as a fragile gift. We are reminded again of Epictetus, the Stoic philosopher who wrote some three centuries later:

> Whenever you grow attached to something, do not act as though it were one of those things that cannot be taken away, but as though it were something like a jar or a crystal goblet, so that when it breaks you will remember what it was like, and not be troubled. So too in life; if you kiss your child, your brother, your friend, never allow your fancy free rein . . . remind yourself that the object of your love is mortal . . . it has been given you for the present, not inseparably, nor for ever, but like a fig, or a cluster of grapes, at a fixed season of the year, and that if you hanker for it in the winter you are a fool.
>
> *(Moral Discourses*, chapter 24)

It is of the greatest interest that those responsible for the final selection of texts in the Hebrew Bible have left in this critique of wisdom, including theological wisdom, from the inside; and it certainly did not happen by oversight. Qoheleth rejects the claim of his colleagues to give a rational account of the world and of the 'work of God' as it impinges on it (8: 16-17); and he does so after a lifetime engaged in the same arduous endeavour:

> All this I have tested by wisdom; I said, 'I will be wise'; but it was far from me. That which is, is far off, and deep, very deep; who can find it out?   (7: 23-4)

The problem remains

The title Ecclesiasticus derives from the Latin and means 'church book'. The reason for the title apparently is that this composition, though not accepted into the Christian canon, was deemed eminently suitable for liturgical use. Its author was a certain Jesus ben

Sira, a Jerusalemite scribe and teacher who wrote in Hebrew in the early decades of the second century BC. He seems to have been familiar with Qoheleth's work and even echoes his sentiments here and there (e.g. Ecclus. 7: 36; 11: 18-19; 18: 22-3). But while he too discourses on human misery (e.g. 40: 1-11) he has little of the intellectual boldness and originality of his predecessor. In fact, he warns against the dangers of speculative thought:

> Seek not what is too difficult for you,
>   nor investigate what is beyond your power.
> Reflect upon what has been assigned to you,
>   for you do not need what is hidden.
> Do not meddle in what is beyond your tasks,
>   for matters too great for human understanding have
>   been shown to you.
> For their hasty judgment has led many astray,
>   and wrong opinion has caused their thoughts to slip.
>   (3: 21-4)

and he may even have had Qoheleth and similar works in mind. A polemical note is also detectable in his strong affirmation of free will and denial that God is in any way responsible for moral incapacity and its toll in human suffering (15: 11-20). Sin is of human not divine origin, deriving as it does from the evil impulse rooted in human nature which, however, can be resisted through prayer and religious observance. Apart from tracing this proclivity to evil back to the first couple (25: 24), a theological position which will be further developed in Jewish and early Christian writings (e.g. Wisd. 2: 23-4; Rom. 5: 12), Ben Sira does not speculate on it or treat it as problematic. He is content to reiterate the received teaching on God's moral governance of the world as a datum of personal experience for the individual who lives by faith and puts his trust in God (e.g. 2: 7-11; 16: 6-23).

Ben Sira agrees with Qoheleth on one point, namely, the exclusion of any form of belief in a life after death as bearing on the intractable problem of the suffering of the innocent. In this respect both adumbrate the Sadducee position over against the Pharisee teaching on the resurrection of the dead. The same position seems to be implied in a saying attributed to the sage Antigonus of Sokho — a contemporary or near-contemporary of Ben Sira — recorded in the tractate *Aboth* of the Mishnah:

> Be not like servants who serve the Master on condition of receiving a gift; but be like servants who serve the Master not on condition of receiving a gift. And let the fear of heaven be on you. (*Mishnah Aboth* 1: 3)

Shortly after Ben Sira wrote his book, however, the Seleucid king Antiochus IV Epiphanes launched the first 'final solution of the Jewish problem' (167 BC) with the proscription of Torah and the establishment of the cult of Zeus in the Jerusalem temple. The ensuing massacre of Jews who remained faithful to the traditional religion — recorded in 1 and 2 Maccabees and reflected in Daniel — raised the problem of divine justice in a more critical way than ever before. It is therefore not surprising that Daniel, written during the crisis to sustain the faith of those suffering persecution, should speak of a final deliverance when those who had died would awake and shine like the brightness of the firmament (Dan. 12: 2-3). The same solution to the problem of overwhelming and apparently triumphant evil is offered in the martyr legends in 2 Maccabees (6: 18 — 7: 42; 14: 37-46). This should not be thought of as an other-worldly solution to an otherwise insoluble problem, but rather an affirmation that, contrary to all appearances, evil and injustice will not have the last word.

The danger of simply denying death, and therefore by-passing the problem which Qoheleth spent a lifetime trying unsuccessfully to solve, is apparent in The Wisdom of Solomon, a treatise written in Greek in Egypt, probably in the late first century BC. True to the tradition of scribal piety in which he stands, the author contrasts the fate of the wicked — in this case apostate Jews — with that of the righteous (1-5), emphasizes the reality of divine judgment (e.g. 11: 15-20), and argues that the suffering of the just is a form of divine discipline (3: 6; 16: 5-14). The new element is the Platonic doctrine of the pre-existence and immortality of souls (2: 23-4; 8: 19-20) leading to an emphasis on spiritual rather than physical death. The just only *seem* to die; in reality, they live on immortal and reign with God:

> The souls of the righteous are in the hands of God,
> and no torment will ever touch them,
> In the eyes of the foolish they seemed to have died,
> and their departure was thought to be an affliction,
> and their going from us to be their destruction;
> but they are at peace. (3: 1–3)

While belief in a life after death, in whatever form it is proposed, cannot be considered a solution to the problem of theodicy and the divine governance of the world, it has often served as such throughout Christian history. The Wisdom of Solomon has something of value to say, but it is well that other voices can speak to us out of that tradition, including the authors of Job and Ecclesiastes.

The first two centuries of Roman rule in Palestine, from Pompey's entrance into Jerusalem in 63 BC to the bloody suppression of the Bar Kochba revolt in AD 135, were marked by crisis and suffering unparalleled — until this century — in the long continuum of Jewish history. Towards the beginning of this period an author, writing under the pseudonym of Baruch, Jeremiah's scribe, spoke for all his people when he prayed, 'Lord Almighty, God of Israel, the soul in anguish and the wearied spirit cry out to thee' (Baruch 3: 1). In general, he follows the Deuteronomic theology according to which Israel is rightly punished for its sins, and specifically for neglecting the prophetic warnings. The second destruction of Jerusalem and its temple in AD 70 precipitated a crisis of faith similar to the first and evoked a passionate search for answers reflected in the literature of that time and the years following. Towards the end of the century an apocalyptic book, appearing under the name of a certain Salathiel, identified with Ezra, struggled with the theological problem why Israel was destined for so much suffering while the nations which oppressed her went unpunished (2 Esd. 3: 28–36). The first answer, given by the angel Uriel in a vision, appealed to divine transcendence rather like the answer Job received in the whirlwind. On this occasion, however, the questioner was not to be satisfied without further probing:

> Why have I been endowed with the power of understanding?
> For I did not wish to inquire about the ways above, but about

those things which we daily experience. (4: 22)

His insistence brought forth a range of alternative explanations: that the present evil age is drawing to a close (the answer of apocalyptic); that, in spite of appearances to the contrary, God still loves his people; that the course of history is predetermined; finally, that suffering is the essential prelude to a blessed immortality (4: 26-37; 5: 40; 6: 1-6; 7: 14). It is safe to assume that the apocalyptic sage's argument with Uriel represents a lively and passionate debate which was going on among scribes and religious leaders at that time.

The questions about divine justice and the moral order of the world raised by the sages of Israel, sharpened by the experience of individual and national suffering and disaster, debated with the greatest freedom in the schools, were therefore by no means put to rest by assurances of a blessed hereafter, in whatever form these may have been offered. It is safe to say that the texts discussed in this chapter, whatever their intellectual limitations, take account of most of the theological options to which little essential has been added in the subsequent centuries. That the problem remains with us is, of course, self-evident. If proof is needed, the reaction to the destruction of a great part of European Judaism in the present century would suffice to show that the responsibility to make sense theologically of 'those things which we daily experience' is not so easily absolved.

4

The Growth of Israel's Legal Tradition

Ordering life by law

The previous chapters have shown how Israelite wisdom aimed at promoting order and maintaining an ethical consensus in the society based on the accumulated experience of the past. In view of this emphasis on justice and order, it would be natural to expect many points of contact with Israel's legal tradition in the different stages of its development. The purpose of the present chapter and the one following is to trace this development and, in doing so, to bring out the different ways in which law and wisdom are related and how they eventually come together.

It should be noted at the outset that the Hebrew word *torah*, generally translated 'law', more properly stands for teaching or instruction. That is to say that, in Old Testament usage, one speaks of the *torah* of a parent, priest, teacher or anyone else qualified to instruct others. In the course of time, however, the word came to refer to the entire legal heritage of Judaism. According to the traditional view, this included not only the law written and delivered at Sinai but also enactments transmitted orally from Moses through various intermediaries to the rabbinic leadership. With the passing of time this too, inevitably, came to be written down, and the result was the Mishnah, a substantial corpus of legal material attributed to Judah the Patriarch towards the end of the second century AD. The process did not, however, stop there, since the Mishnah continued to be expanded and commented on, the final product being the Talmud. In its shorter Palestinian and longer Babylonian versions, this immense collection of legal and narrative material was essentially complete by the fifth century AD. While the word *torah* continued to be used of Pentateuchal law, and of the Pentateuch as a whole, it can also refer in Judaism to the entire corpus of written and (originally) oral law.

The Jewish tradition of referring to the first five books of the Bible as Torah raises an issue which has some relevance for our present theme. For, in spite of the great number of laws which they contain (the traditional count is 613), these books would more naturally be construed as a narrative from creation to the death of Moses. We need not go into the origin of this usage, attested in early Christian writings and in Josephus, except to say that it occurs unequivocally no earlier than the second century BC. It immediately draws our attention to the context in which the laws are presented. More specifically, it suggests that their significance and function are to be understood in the light of historical events, and especially the history of God's relations with his people. If, moreover, both law and narrative can together be described as *torah* — in the sense of teaching or instruction — a further implication would be that law is, in a certain sense, subsumed under wisdom. Thus the teacher Ben Sira, writing about 180 BC, describes the Jewish philosopher — the seeker after wisdom — as in the first place a student of the law (Ecclus. 39: 1). He goes further and identifies the law as divine wisdom sent on earth to instruct humankind (24: 1-29). When his grandson came to write an introduction to the book about half a century later, he remained true to this perspective by describing the law as the first and principal part of Israel's intellectual heritage.

Writings which have survived from the Second Temple period — whether biblical texts like Chronicles and Psalms or post-biblical writings like Jubilees and the Qumran scrolls — testify to the central place of Torah in Jewish intellectual life, private piety and public worship; and so it has remained to the present. The author of Ps. 19, to take one example, uses a variety of synonyms to describe the effects of the study and observance of Torah:

> The law of Yahweh is perfect,
>> reviving the soul;
> The testimony of Yahweh is sure,
>> making wise the simple;
> The precepts of Yahweh are right,
>> rejoicing the heart;
> The commandment of Yahweh is pure,
>> enlightening the eyes . . .   (Ps. 19: 7–8)

Torah, in other words, is a source of life, wisdom, joy, and enlightenment. Though well known, this should be emphasized precisely because it has been so subject to misunderstanding. Whether in terms of the sharp contrast between law and gospel, or between 'dead works' and justification by faith, the peculiar Jewish concern to regulate life by law has been routinely misrepresented as legalism — what Julius Wellhausen a century ago dismissed as 'a petty scheme of salvation'. A concern for law can, certainly, degenerate into legalism and formalism, but such a tendency is found in Christian thought and practice, as well as in other religious traditions.

The concentration on Torah which pervades the piety of Second Temple Judaism can be traced back, in good part, to Deuteronomy. As we shall see later in the chapter, this book represents, in this respect as in others, the great divide between Israel and Judaism. Most critical scholars connect it in some way with the reforms of Josiah (640-609 BC), the last great king of Judah, with further expansions and additions from the time of the Babylonian exile and possibly later. We find for the first time in Deuteronomy the word *torah* used not of an individual stipulation of law — as previously — but of a collection or corpus of laws (1: 5; 4: 44; etc.). Understood in this sense, *torah* is said to constitute for Israel what wisdom is to those nations which boast an ancient and well established scribal tradition:

Behold, I have taught you statutes and ordinances . . . Keep them and do them; for that will be your wisdom and understanding in the sight of the peoples, who, when they hear all these statutes, will say, 'Surely this great nation is a wise and understanding people.'   (4: 5-6)

In the manner of the sages, the author sees life made up of choices and decisions. He can therefore present the law, in the context of the teaching of the Two Ways, as a guide to choosing and deciding well:

See, I have set before you this day life and good, death and evil. If you obey the commandments of Yahweh your God which I command you this day . . . then you shall live and multiply.
(30: 15-16)

The fact that the speaker throughout is Moses is also a constant reminder to the audience that this wisdom is associated with the memory of events to which Israel owes its existence as a people.

This last point is important for understanding law as the means of defining the kind of community Israel was destined to be. Deuteronomy is presented to the reader as the valedictory of Moses, an address delivered to the people in the wilderness on the last day of his life. The book, however, contains many indications, of which the account of Moses's death and burial is the most obvious, that in its present form it cannot have come from his hand. In the course of this address 'Moses' presents to the assembly not so much a law code as a programme for life in the land which they were to enter after his death (chapters 12-26). A close reading of this programme, referring back to the collection of laws in Ex. 20-3, will suggest that it was not only later in date than these laws but, in some important respects, intended to supersede them. Ex. 20: 24-5, for example, assumes that animal sacrifice may be carried on at different places so long as certain conditions are fulfilled. Deut. 12: 5-14, on the other hand, stipulates that only at the one place designated by Yahweh is sacrifice legitimate. Since law is meant to correspond to actual situations, and since these situations are subject to change with the passing of time, this is no more than we would expect. In Israel, however, the acknowledgement of change and adaptation was always tempered by the need to relate law *as a totality* to certain events in which the presence and action of God were discerned. Hence all the laws, including those in Deuteronomy, are assumed to derive from the self-manifestation of Israel's God at Sinai/Horeb.

The precise understanding of how this was thought to happen is rendered practically impossible by successive editing, corresponding to centuries of reflection, of the basic Sinai narrative (Ex. 19: 1 – Num. 10: 28). This entire section, which makes up about one third of the Pentateuch, is framed by the account of the wandering in the wilderness, beginning after the crossing of the sea (Ex. 15: 22) and continuing on after the people leave Sinai (Num. 10: 29 – Deut. 34: 12). Other versions of Israel's wanderings have come down to us which are silent about the giving of the law even when they mention a stay at Sinai (Num. 33: 15-16; Judg. 11: 12-23). Yet other traditions (e.g. Deut. 33: 8-11) speak of the administration of justice elsewhere in 'that great and terrible wilderness'. All of this has suggested to some scholars that the entire Sinai narrative had an independent existence before being inserted into the mainstream of the story. For our purposes it is not essential to decide on the merits of this hypothesis. If we restrict our attention to the Sinai story itself, it will be difficult to avoid the impression that it has grown to its present dimensions by a gradual process of expansion. Suffice it to note how often Moses goes up and down the mountain as he mediates between God and the people.

According to one strand of this narrative, it appears that Yahweh gave the entire law to Moses who at once promulgated it (Ex. 19: 7-8; 24: 3). This strand is, however, juxtaposed with another according to which only the Ten Commandments were promulgated there and then (Ex. 20: 1 cf. Deut. 4: 10; 5: 4 – 5, 22) while the detailed stipulations of law were communicated to Moses alone, with the understanding that he would promulgate them at a later time (Ex. 20: 21; 24: 7). The author of Deuteronomy has exploited this delay in order to present an updated version of these stipulations, one designed for the new situation which confronted Israel in his day.

Law in early Israel

In its several redactions Deuteronomy represents a landmark in the development and consolidation of Israel's legal traditions. Probing behind Deuteronomy towards the reconstruction of earlier stages in this development is, unfortunately, no easy task and much will remain uncertain and subject to revision. The biblical traditions themselves attest to the importance of the nomadic period of Israel's early history. Nomadic societies are based on blood relations and organized in kinship groups, with the tribe divided into clusters of closely related family units or households. Within his own 'extended family' the father or patriarch was the sole administrator of justice and exercised wide discretionary power. In cases which concerned the entire kinship group, however, decisions were in the hands of the tribal elders to whom the customary law of the group, orally transmitted, was entrusted. It seems reasonable to assume that something like this mode of organization, which has survived down to the present in 'primitive' societies, obtained among those Hebrew tribes whose original home was in the Sinai or the wilderness south of the Dead Sea and who came to form Israel after their settlement in the land of Canaan.

Some of the most ancient features of the administration of law in Israel can best be explained as survivals from the nomadic period — for example, the blood feud and the principle of corporate liability. The former may be exemplified by the savage chant of Lamech, descendant of Cain, in Gen. 4: 23–4:

> I have slain a man for wounding me,
>   a young man for striking me.
> If Cain is avenged sevenfold,
>   truly Lamech seventy-sevenfold!

The principle of corporate liability, which gradually lost its place in the administration of justice, is reflected in the old formula about God visiting the iniquity of the fathers on the children to the third and fourth generation (Ex. 34: 7; Num. 14: 18). With the passing of time such ideas and formulations inevitably underwent modification. The law of talion (an eye for an eye, a tooth for a tooth, etc.) is best explained as an attempt to control indiscriminate vengeance on the part of the blood-group by applying the principle of equity — in the sense of *only* an eye for an eye, *only* a tooth for a tooth. Since it is found in the Code of Hammurapi and even in Roman law it is probably not of nomadic origin.

Practices associated with the blood feud survived only in special applications of the law of sanctuary, dealing with homicide (Num.

35: 16-21; Deut. 19: 12-13). By the time of Deuteronomy, the group was held responsible only in the exceptional cases of idolatry and homicide (Deut. 13: 6-11; 21: 1-9). Significantly, both deal with acts done in secret when, therefore, the perpetrator cannot be identified. The idea of collective guilt was eventually repudiated as inconsistent with the individual's claim to justice: 'the fathers shall not be put to death for the children, nor shall the children be put to death for the fathers; every man shall be put to death for his own sin' (Deut. 24: 16 cf. 2 Kgs. 14: 6 and Jer. 31: 29). The decalogue reflects this advance by limiting the extent of culpability along the line of the generations to 'those who hate me' (Ex. 20: 5; Deut. 5: 9).

In a broader sense early Israel, whatever its remote origins, was a traditional society, which implies that norms for conduct were determined by appeal to the wisdom of the group accumulated over centuries. Here, too, analogy may be a useful means of understanding how a legal tradition and judicial procedures develop in this kind of social context. Among the Ibo of Nigeria, for example, disputes in law are settled by tribal elders dressed for the occasion in the robes and masks of ancestor-spirits; while among the neighbouring Anang tribe the timely citing of a proverbial saying during a judicial hearing can have a decisive effect. While the cultures are, of course, widely different, in Israel too the elders, as the depositories of tribal wisdom, played the decisive role in legal matters. They were the ones deemed best able to judge what kind of conduct was or was not consonant with the ethos of the group. The typical form of case law, which states the facts in the protasis ('when a man does x') and the legal consequences in the apodosis ('then y must happen'), is really a special case of group experience applied to the solution of specific problems. In this respect it is analogous to those proverbial sayings discussed in a previous chapter in which a certain kind of behaviour is linked with specific consequences. In such a society, then, law is simply a specialization of tribal wisdom.

Archaic features are also apparent in the formulation of legal principles which originated in an oral culture. Such, for example, is the sentence of law in Gen. 9: 6 which, literally translated, runs as follows:

> The shedder of the blood of a man —
> By a man his blood shall be shed.

Similar in form are the death penalty sentences which designate the subject with the participle:

> Whoever strikes (literally, 'the one striking') a man so that he dies shall be put to death . . . .
> Whoever strikes his father or his mother shall be put to death.
> Whoever steals a man . . . shall be put to death.
> Whoever curses his father or his mother shall be put to death.
> (Ex. 21: 12–17)

This too is an ancient formulation which has found its way into the earliest extant collection of Israelite laws (Ex. 20: 23 – 23: 19). It is, of course, quite different from the case law referred to a moment ago since it enunciates a general principle which is to be applied, with the necessary clarifications and distinctions, to specific cases. We shall see that it belongs to the same class of categoric legal statement as the more familiar 'you shall not kill' formulation in the decalogue.

If, as noted above, case law is in some respects comparable with proverbial wisdom, categoric law exemplified in the decalogue has analogies with the admonitions and instructions of the sages. In a previous chapter we saw how the instruction makes frequent use of the imperative: 'Do not plan evil against your neighbour . . . Do not contend with a man for no reason . . . Do not envy a man of violence' (Prov. 3: 29-31). While the grammatical form is not quite identical in Hebrew, the similarity between this kind of admonition and the negative commandments of the decalogue has led several scholars to suggest that the latter also derive from the ancient deposit of tribal wisdom and embody the ethos of the kinship group. This may be true in a very general way, but the hypothesis would in any case have to allow for later elaborations and developments. Some of these we shall see at a later point in the chapter.

The Covenant Code (Ex. 20: 23 – 23: 19)

The oldest collection of Israelite laws, described later in the narrative as 'the covenant book' (Ex. 24: 7), is presented as given to Moses at Sinai. It is widely agreed, however, that since it presupposes an agrarian economy, it cannot be earlier than the settlement in Canaan. It is even possible that many of its stipulations were borrowed from Canaanite common law, though unfortunately no such laws have survived. Moreover, the cultic laws which the code contains are, if anything, anti-Canaanite. The tradition identifies it with the law book read by Joshua during a covenant ceremony at Shechem, an important centre in the pre-state period about forty miles due north of Jerusalem (Jos. 8: 30-5; 24: 1-28 cf. Deut. 27). This has been taken to imply that, in whatever form it then existed, it served as the law for a federation of tribes organized around the Shechem sanctuary in the period preceding the rise of the monarchy. At the very least, it contains nothing which obliges us to date it any later.

There can be no doubt, then, that this collection existed independently prior to its incorporation into the Sinai narrative. The arrangement of different kinds of legal material in it makes it equally clear that it reached its present form only after a considerable passage of time. It will be noted, for example, that laws governing idolatry and the construction of altars precede the title at Ex. 21: 1, and that the collection also ends with cultic legislation (23: 10-19). Such an arrangement suggests the intent of providing a civic code with a religious framework. It will be seen, too, that the laws are not all of a kind. The death penalty sentences in the participial form, presented earlier, interrupt a collection of miscellaneous case laws (21: 1 – 22: 17) which are quite different in form from the series of laws in the imperative which follows (22: 18 – 23: 19). Since case law (the term 'casuistic' is also often used) is the standard form of legal enactment in Israel and the ancient Near East, it is reasonable to infer that the sixteen laws of this kind with their explanatory codicils formed a separate collection illustrative of early Israelite common law.

Until the beginning of this century the laws in the Old Testament were the only ones known to us from the ancient Near East. It was therefore impossible to assess claims made by both Jews and Christians that biblical law was uniquely humanitarian in character or inspired by a high ideal of justice unattested elsewhere. The absence of comparative material also made it very difficult to get a precise idea of the form and function of the different kinds of legal material found in the Old Testament. Then in 1901 the column inscribed with the laws of Hammurapi king of Babylon was discovered in the Elamite city of Susa, and since then a good cross-section of legal material has come to light from Mesopotamia and Asia Minor, most of which dates from the second millennium BC or earlier. While in no case is it possible to derive Israelite law directly from this earlier material, it is now quite clear that early Israel inherited a legal tradition which can be traced back to the Sumerian city states of the late third millennium BC.

One noteworthy feature of several of these collections, including the laws of Hammurapi, is that they are provided with a prologue and epilogue. The laws of Ur-nammu, founder of the third dynasty of Ur towards the end of the third millennium BC, are introduced by an address of the king listing the benefits he had conferred on his people, of which the most important was maintaining justice and protecting the disadvantaged:

> The orphan was not delivered up to the rich man,
> The widow was not delivered up to the mighty man,
> The man of one shekel was not delivered up to the man of one
>   mina. (lines 162–8)

The same kind of statement occurs as a preface to the laws of Lipit-ishtar of the Sumerian city of Isin and, at greater length, in the prologue to the laws of Hammurapi. In addition, the last two are rounded off with an epilogue which stipulates the setting up of the stele on which the laws were written and enjoins that all are to have free access to it. The code of Hammurapi also prohibits any alteration to the laws and ends with curses and blessings to ensure that they are respected and obeyed.

The laws in the Old Testament, and especially those in Deuteronomy, are also provided with such prefaces and conclusions. The most obvious difference is that the Israelite laws are presented within a continuous historical context, implying that it is this history which gives the law its meaning for Israel.

A study of the Mesopotamian laws also raises the difficult question of the nature, origin, and function of such collections. The term law code is widely used, but if by this designation we mean something analogous to the Napoleonic Code it would clearly be inappropriate. None of the collections, not even that of Hammurapi with its 282 paragraphs, covers all significant aspects of public life or even comes close to being comprehensive. The sixteen paragraphs of the Covenant Code (Ex. 21: 1-11, 18-36; 22: 1-17), even when augmented with the categoric statements about cult and other matters, cover only a small area of public life. Some have thought that the purpose was to give samples of early Israelite legislation, but it seems more likely that they were intended to provide guidance on more difficult and problematic cases of law.

It has also been suggested that the Mesopotamian collections may have been compiled from royal edicts issued at the beginning of a reign or at seven-year intervals during it. Such edicts, like that of a later king of Babylon named Ammisaduqa which is extant, dealt only with exceptional matters such as the manumission of slaves and the forgiveness of debts. This will remind us of the Old Testament laws governing the sabbatical and jubilee year (Ex. 23: 10-11; Lev. 25) and the stipulation that the law be read publicly every seven years (Deut. 31: 10-13). It is also worth noting that the practice of re-issuing and re-validating laws at the beginning of a reign continued down into the Persian period.

Whatever their origin, these collections must have served to guide judges in handing down decisions in more difficult and complex cases. In due course they would have passed into the hands of scribes and scholars who were responsible for their interpretation. Evidence of the activity of these legal scholars can be seen in the amplifications of the individual laws in the Covenant Code. Some of these are explanatory, e.g. in the law which stipulates that a creditor must return a garment taken in pledge between sundown and sunrise:

> If ever you take your neighbour's garment in pledge, you shall restore it to him before the sun goes down; *for that is his only covering, it is his mantle for his body*; *in what else shall he sleep?*   (Ex. 22: 26-7)

In other cases the expansion provides motivation either of a general ethical kind or by reference to specifically Israelite traditions. An example like the following provides an important clue to the relationship between the laws and the narrative tradition:

> You shall not oppress a stranger; *you know the heart of a stranger, for you were strangers in the land of Egypt*. (Ex. 23: 9)

We shall see that the role of these legal scholars would become increasingly important in the later stages of the history.

A comparison of the laws in Mesopotamian collections with those of the Covenant Code does not support the view that the latter are in all respects more advanced and humanitarian in character. Nor does it substantiate the liberal idea of a progressively more enlightened approach to penal legislation. The death penalty occurs much more often in early Israelite legislation, for example, than in the Sumerian laws where capital sentence is reserved to the crown. In the laws of Eshnunna the owner of a rogue ox which kills someone is fined, whereas in the Covenant Code he is sentenced to death (Ex. 21: 29). The Code of Hammurapi provides better protection to a woman divorced by her husband than does early Israelite legislation. Where the Covenant Code stands apart is with respect to its historical context and its evolution — seen especially in the expansions — towards a more comprehensive guide for living.

In point of fact, the relative degree of enlightenment reflected in laws is generally a function of the stage of social and political evolution reached by the society in which the laws are in force. In societies which still preserve a tribal structure, for example, a case of homicide is generally settled by the blood feud. In this respect early Israel is no different from the society reflected in the Homeric poems. With the passage from tribal society to state, however, law codes come into existence which reserve judgment in such important matters to the state. In Mesopotamia this stage of evolution occurred no later than the second millennium while in Greece we have to wait until the seventh century BC for the first written state law, that of Draco of Athens, almost exactly contemporary with the promulgation of the Deuteronomic law in Israel. We have already seen that in Deuteronomy the principle of corporate liability, characteristic of a tribal structure, survives only in the exceptional cases of homicide and apostasy where the perpetrator remains undetected.

We must now look a little more closely at the way in which the stipulations of the Covenant Code are formulated. The title identifies the case laws as 'ordinances' and the context distinguishes these from the kind of categoric or apodictic statements found in the decalogue which are called simply 'words' (Ex. 20: 1; 24: 3). The first of the sixteen ordinances provides a good example of how case law was formulated and some indication as to how it was administered. We may set it out as follows:

> When you buy a Hebrew slave, he shall serve six years, and in the seventh he shall go out free, for nothing.
> 1) If he comes in single, he shall go out single;
> 2) If he comes in married, then his wife shall go out with him.
> 3) If his master gives him a wife and she bears him sons or daughters, the wife and her children shall be her master's and he shall go out alone.
> 4) But if the slave plainly says, 'I love my master, my wife, and my children; I will not go out free,' then his master shall bring him to God, and he shall bring him to the door or the doorpost; and his master shall bore his ear through with an awl; and he shall serve him for life.   (Ex. 21: 2-6)

The protasis gives the facts of the case, i.e., the purchase of a Hebrew slave, and the apodosis the legal consequences, i.e., mandatory release in the seventh year after purchase. As is generally the case, however, special circumstances call for more specific rulings, and these are laid out in subordinate clauses. In this instance there are four: (1) a slave who is single at the time of purchase and remains single; (2) a slave who is married at the time of purchase; (3) one who marries after becoming the property of his master; (4) one in the third category who does not wish to separate from his wife and children. Only this last calls for a special jurisdiction since it results legally in a state of perpetual slavery and therefore contradicts the basic intent of the law. A symbolic act must therefore be carried out at the tribal sanctuary ('before God') – the piercing of the slave's ear as the organ of hearing and obeying – certainly in the presence of higher judicial authority.

If we compare this ordinance with the Deuteronomic reformulation (Deut. 15: 12-18) we shall have some idea of the development of the legal tradition in Israel. There is the same basic stipulation, presented under the rubric of the year of release (15: 1), with the interesting exception that the female slave is given explicit mention (vss. 12, 17). The law is now silent on the eventuality of the slave having to choose between his freedom and abandoning his wife and children, perpetual slavery resulting only when the slave in question opts to remain out of attachment to his master. It is also stipulated that the master must provide liberally for his manumitted slave in the year of release. Motivation is supplied with reference to Israel's common memory of slavery in Egypt, a feature which is also found in the Covenant Code as we have seen.

It was this kind of case law which formed the basis for the daily administration of justice in Israel, as elsewhere in the Near East. From the Old Testament narrative as well as the laws some idea can be formed as to how this operated: such things as the administering and taking of oaths (crucial in a society without a police force), the role of witnesses, the practice of the ordeal and the like. The normal location was the city gate, meaning the large plaza which formed an essential part of the gate complex known from the excavation of Bronze Age and Iron Age sites. A good example occurs towards the end of Ruth when her nearest kinsman is given first refusal of Naomi's property and of the right to marry Ruth which went with it. The text describes the gathering of the principals in the case:

> Boaz went up to the gate and sat down there; and behold, the next of kin, of whom Boaz had spoken, came by. So Boaz said, 'Turn aside, friend; sit down here'; and he turned aside and sat down. And he took ten men of the elders of the city, and said, 'Sit down here'; so they sat down. (4: 1-2)

The elders clearly played an important part in the day to day administration of justice, and it was they, apparently, who appointed the judges in the period before the rise of the monarchy (e.g. 1 Sam. 8: 4-5). A good example of the latter would be Samuel who, as circuit judge, went from place to place administering the law at the local sanctuaries (1 Sam. 7: 15-17). The office could, it seems, be hereditary (1 Sam. 8: 1-3). The same substructure remained after the passage to monarchy, the major innovation being the creation of a central judiciary or court of appeals in Jerusalem (Deut. 17: 8-13; cf. 2 Chr. 19: 5-11). The several allusions in the Pentateuch to Moses delegating authority (e.g. Ex. 18: 13-26; Deut. 1: 9-18) probably reflect this important institution. True to the ancient Near Eastern ideal of the monarch as the custodian of justice, there was, ideally at least, free access to the king as the final arbiter of disputed cases or of those in which an alleged miscarriage of justice had taken place (e.g. 2 Sam. 14: 4-20; 1 Kgs. 3: 16-28).

The Ten Commandments

The Covenant Code contains, in addition to case laws, different kinds of categoric statements or legal principles which must now be considered. The so-called 'law of the altar' which prefaces the entire collection (20: 23-6) is, formally, more like an instruction. It contains imperatives, includes a promise of divine blessing, and provides reasons for constructing altars in the way prescribed. It therefore hardly qualifies as law in the strict sense of the term. The death penalty series (21: 12-17) has already been introduced as a distinct kind of categoric or apodictic enactment similar to the curse-formulations occurring elsewhere in the Pentateuch (Deut. 27: 15-26). In the last part of the collection (23: 1-19) there is also a prevalence of mixed forms, with commands in the positive and negative, exhortation and motivation, all much more reminiscent of a catechism than a law code.

We noted earlier that the Sinai narrative distinguishes between 'ordinances' (the case laws) and 'words' and that the decalogue is introduced as 'words', which can perhaps be taken to connote legal principles. It is understood that these are universally binding as a direct expression of the divine will for Israel. The decalogue is only one of several such series of categoric statements in the Pentateuch. In the Covenant Code itself, besides the five formulaic death sentences discussed earlier, there is a series of commands mostly in the negative (22: 18-23) and a list of prohibitives dealing with the administration of justice (23: 1-3, 6-9), both of which may be derived from originally independent decalogues. The series promulgated after the apostasy of the Golden Calf (34: 13-26) also appears to be a decalogue. In the present state of the text it is, in fact, identified as such (34: 28). The litany of curses which concludes the covenant-making in Deuteronomy (27: 15-26) lists twelve infractions and is therefore a dodecalogue. The practice of listing legal enactments or principles of law in a short series, with a preference for ten or twelve, is therefore well attested and no doubt ancient.

Attempts have been made to identify a model for the decalogue outside Israel which might help to solve the much debated problem of its date and origin. Many scholars have been impressed by certain structural similarities between Hittite vassal treaties, discovered at the ancient Hittite capital of Boghazköy near Ankara in Turkey, and the way in which covenants are made and renewed in the Old Testament. Since these treaties date from the fourteenth and thirteenth centuries BC, the analogy also seemed to have the advantage of confirming the great antiquity of these biblical formulations. The treaties in question begin with a preamble in which the suzerain identifies himself, and continue with an account of past benefits (real or fictitious) conferred on the vassal, obviously with a view to motivating him to remain faithful to his allegiance. There then follow the stipulations of the treaty together with provisions for its display and public reading. It concludes with a list of gods as witnesses and a series of blessings and curses contingent on its observance and violation respectively.

Since something of the same structure can be detected in certain Old Testament passages dealing with law and covenant, these treaty texts have been seen to provide some important clues to the origin and date of the Israelite covenant idea. The analogy has certainly proved to be stimulating and valuable, not least in highlighting the political dimensions of early Israelite religious thinking, but not all the claims made for it have been sustained. It can be shown, for example, that the structure in question is not confined to Hittite international treaties of the late second millennium but is also a feature of Assyrian treaties roughly contemporary with Jeremiah and the book of Deuteronomy. Not all the proposed similarities, moreover, hold up under close scrutiny, and certainly not with respect to the decalogue. The prologue, 'I am Yahweh your God who brought you out of the land of Egypt, out of the house of bondage', is similar in neither form nor length to the preambles and historical introductions to the treaties. The stipulations are also, for the most part, couched in a different way, and there is no parallel in the treaties to the series of ten or twelve.

Other analogies which have been proposed − e.g., lists of misdeeds disavowed by the faithful in the Egyptian Books of the Dead and Assyrian catalogues of sins − are also wide of the mark. We have to conclude that, in the present state of our knowledge, the decalogue has to be explained as a purely internal development in Israel.

In an important study published in 1934 under the title 'The Origins of Israelite Law', the German scholar Albrecht Alt argued that the categoric or apodictic laws, as distinct from case law, originated in Israelite worship and were recited during the autumnal festival of Sukkoth (Tabernacles) when the covenant between Yahweh and the people was solemnly renewed. That the laws, including the decalogue, were transmitted in this way is clearly attested:

> Moses commanded them, 'At the end of every seven years, at the set time of the year of release, at the feast of booths, when all Israel comes to appear before Yahweh your God at the place which he will choose, you shall read this law before all Israel in their hearing.' (Deut. 31: 10-11)

This practice of public reading continued down into the late biblical period (Neh. 7: 73 − 8: 8). One of the major functions of cult in Israel was to keep on re-affirming the ethical implications of the covenant-relationship. There can be no doubt, then, that the cult incorporated the law in this way, but it is quite another matter to argue that it somehow generated this form of legal pronouncement. It seems more likely that several factors have to be reckoned with, cultic recital being only one of them.

A further aspect comes into view when we note that the decalogue has close affinity with the ethical teaching of the prophets. Where the prophets under the monarchy denounce their contemporaries, their accusations are, for the most part, highly specific. They can also be shown to correspond in many instances to equally specific points of law. When Amos, for example, condemns those who sleep on garments taken in pledge (2: 8) he is referring to the law in the Covenant Code, quoted earlier, which obliges a creditor to return a pawned garment between sundown and sunrise (Ex. 22: 26-7). We can, at the same time, detect a generalizing tendency in prophetic preaching whereby the essence of the laws is expressed in a brief and compendious way. An example would be the much-quoted text from Micah (6: 8):

> He has shown you, O man, what is good;
> and what does Yahweh require of you
> but to do justice, and to love kindness,
> and to walk humbly with your God?

When, on the other hand, an equally broad description of a faithless community is called for, we hear unmistakeable echoes of the decalogue:

> There is swearing, lying, killing, stealing, and committing
> adultery;
> they break all bounds and murder follows murder.
>
> (Hos. 4: 2)

> Will you steal, murder, commit adultery, swear falsely, burn incense to Baal, and go after other gods that you have not known, and then come and stand before me in this house? (Jer. 7: 9-10)

This might be thought to imply that the decalogue was already familiar by the time of the prophets. But in view of the different order in which the offences occur here, together with the fact that all of them can be found in series other than the decalogue, it seems better to conclude that prophetic preaching influenced the final form of the decalogue. It may therefore be tentatively proposed that this great compendium of the moral life was the result of a selection from older lists which reached its final form in Exodus and Deuteronomy by way of prophetic preaching.

Comparison of the two versions of the decalogue (Ex. 20: 1-17 and Deut. 5: 6-21) leads to the conclusion that the individual stipulations — all save two of which are in the negative — have been expanded in the course of usage. Thus, the prohibition against making images is rounded off with a theological reason: the exclusive claim which the God of Israel lays on his devotees. The sabbath command is enjoined in one case (Ex. 20: 11) with reference to creation and in the other (Deut. 5: 14-15) on humanitarian grounds — to provide respite for servants — and with specific reference to the tradition of Israel in Egypt. The former is characteristic of the Priestly Source in the Pentateuch (P) while the latter is typically Deuteronomic. Motivation is also provided for honouring parents — in both cases to secure lasting possession of the land. This too is a typically Deuteronomic theme. Whatever the original form of the tenth word, it is noticeable that in Deuteronomy the wife is no longer listed as, so to speak, one of the household effects, the possession of the husband. As with the reformulation of the slavery laws, this may represent a step forward in acknowledging the dignity of the woman as a person in her own right.

These expansions are also found in the other series and throw valuable light on the way the law functioned in Israel. They also help to bring out the theological significance of law as related to a certain understanding of the character of Israel's God and the common memory through which Israel affirmed and preserved its identity and way of life.

Deuteronomy: the watershed

Towards the end of the second millennium BC the loose federation of tribes which constituted Israel found itself driven to elect first military overlords and then kings in order to survive the Philistine menace. It was obvious from the beginning that the passage to monarchy would impose a severe strain on the tribal organization, its various substructures and the ethos which sustained it. Ideally, the monarchy and its attendant institutions existed to support this ethos and were subject to the laws. Whatever its historical character, the story of the seer Nathan taking David to task for adultery reflects this conviction (2 Sam. 12: 1-15). Later in the same narrative Amnon, first in line to succeed David, attempts to seduce his half-sister Tamar and is warned by her that 'such a thing is not done in Israel' (13: 12). In the following century Ahab, ruler of the Northern Kingdom, planned to extend the palace grounds in Samaria and, to that end, offered to buy out a landowner who had a vineyard adjacent to the palace. Despite the favourable terms of the contract, the latter refused on the traditional grounds of the inalienability of family property, a decision in which Ahab clearly felt he had no alternative but to acquiesce (1 Kgs. 21: 1-4). Such episodes, which would be difficult to parallel in contemporary monarchies, attest to the capacity of a legal tradition laid down in the pre-state period to survive in a very different and less congenial atmosphere.

The outcome of the dispute between Ahab and Naboth, with the latter a victim of judicial murder and the former in possession of his subject's property, may serve to show how this situation of tension, left to itself, would be resolved. Inevitably Israel was drawn into conformity with the model of statehood provided by those Canaanite city-states, including Jerusalem, which survived the Israelite takeover. Support of a state bureaucracy, which included the cult, and of large-scale building projects, which included a great national shrine, imposed an intolerable economic burden on the small farmers who worked the land. A standing army took the place of the tribal levy and, together with forced labour, became another source of discontent. Enclosure of peasant land and absentee landlordism also contributed to corroding a traditional way of life, its ethos and the religion which sustained it.

It is against this background, roughly sketched, that we have to assess the social role of those prophets who operated independently of state institutions. Together with other groups mentioned here and there in the record (e.g. Nazirites and Rechabites) they represented a conservative reaction to changes which threatened a traditional way of life. Hence the frequent allusion in prophetic books to Israel's origins and the failure of their contemporaries to honour ancient commitments. While most of the prophets had very limited success in directly influencing the society of their day, their ethical teaching found expression in Deuteronomy and thus remained authoritative and normative even after the loss of national independence.

The title of Deuteronomy derives from the Greek *deuteros nomos*, a second law, which in its turn derives from Deut. 17: 18 where it is said that the king must write for himself 'a copy of this law' to keep by him. The book does, however, contain a second law in that many of the stipulations in Deut. 12-26 – the legal nucleus – are updatings of laws in the Covenant Code. The title is therefore not inappropriate, whatever the intentions of the Greek translators may have been. In Hebrew the book is introduced as words of Moses and can be described as his valedictory, being addressed to all Israel on the last day of his life. With entry into the land to follow immediately after his death, a new and quite different epoch would be ushered in.

The reader will note how the superscription (1: 1-5) has been expanded in different ways in the course of the book's transmission. The addition of topographical detail (vv. 1b-2, 4) links that moment in time with the giving of the law at Sinai (here referred to as Horeb) and the even older tradition of judicial activity at the oasis of Kadesh in the Sinai peninsula. The precise date (v. 3) is characteristic not of Deuteronomy but of the Priestly Source (P). Together with the account of Moses's death from the same source at the end of the book (32: 48-52; 34: 1, 7-9), it provides a valuable clue to the incorporation of Deuteronomy into the mainline narrative of the Pentateuch. In this protracted introduction Moses is presented as a scribe who undertakes to explain the law (v. 5). The fact that we have to wait eleven chapters for such legal exposition is only one indication that the book reached its present form after a long and complex process of transmission.

We must note, too, that the introduction alludes to a law which requires interpretation, one therefore capable of generating commentary. The term is consistent with other indications that Deuteronomy marks the first appearance of a canonical text: the injunction not to add to or subtract from it (4: 2; 12: 32) , the solemn appeal to witnesses (4: 26), the stipulation about the king's copy (17: 18-19) and the appending of blessings and curses (27-28). All of these are reminiscent of the way international treaties were drawn up and validated, and signal the intent to publish an authoritative document.

The superscription alerts us to the composite nature of the book, as we have just seen. Other features pointing in the same direction will emerge as we read on, including titles, change of subject matter, change from singular to plural, and the like. We are promised legal interpretation in the opening verses, but what follows is a historical summary of events between Horeb and arrival in Moab just east of the Jordan (1: 6 – 3: 29). A little later there is another solemn introduction, again with topographical expansions, to a collection of laws (4: 44-9). There follows the decalogue (5: 6-21) and, eventually, the ordinances (12-26) with a great deal of homiletic or catechetical instruction interspersed. This law book, as we may provisionally designate it, is rounded off with a ratification of the covenant together with blessings and curses and a closing address of Moses (27-30). The last section (31-4) is the conclusion to the Pentateuch as a whole and has no intrinsic connection with Deuteronomy itself.

It may be convenient to set out the structure of the book as follows:

1: 1-5	Superscription
1: 6 – 3: 29	Historical summary: from Horeb to Moab
4: 1-40	Concluding address: lessons from the history
4: 41-3	Appendix: cities of refuge
4: 44-9	Superscription
5	Address of Moses presenting the decalogue
6-11	Commentary on the first word of the decalogue
12-26	The Deuteronomic law book
27	Ratification of the covenant
28: 1 – 29: 1	Blessings and curses
29: 2 – 30: 20	Final address of Moses
31-4	Conclusion to the Pentateuch

While it is no longer possible to reconstruct exactly the stages by which the book reached its present form, an earlier version probably began with the introduction at 4: 44 and ended with the long list of curses in chapter 28 and the solemn finale at 29: 1. This First Temple composition was then expanded during the Babylonian exile with the long historical introduction, its conclusion, and the final address. It will be noted that these last two abound in references to exile and, in fact, sound like sermons delivered to the exiled communities. A further indication is that only here are curse and blessing presented as successive stages, and therefore as holding out hope for the future.

The modern study of the book has taken its point of departure in the correspondence between the religious reforms of Josiah (640–609 BC) and the cultic legislation of Deuteronomy, especially the disestablishment of the provincial sanctuaries (called 'high places' in the Old Testament) and the proscription of pagan cult practices. According to the narrator, these reforms were precipitated by the finding of a law book during repair work on the temple during the eighteenth year of the king's reign (2 Kgs. 22: 8). It may be surmised, however, that the very fact of repairing the temple pointed to a movement of religious renewal already underway, a surmisal which is confirmed by the author of Chronicles who dates the beginning of the reform six years earlier than the finding of the book (2 Chr. 34: 3–7). The book in question was certainly Deuteronomy, or so the author wished it to be understood. But whether the account of its discovery is historical and, if so, whether it had really been lost or, rather, 'planted' by the reform party for their own purposes and with the best of intentions, are questions which can no longer be answered with certainty.

The movement for religious renewal which gathered strength during Josiah's reign went together with Judah's bid for independence from the Assyrians after more than a century of vassalage. This attempt would have had a chance of success only after the death of Ashurbanipal, the last effective king of Assyria, in 627 BC, and it is not without significance that the Chronicler dates the religious reforms to within a year of that time.

It should also be noted that reforms of this kind had been going on intermittently throughout the history of Judah from very early days (1 Kgs. 15: 12–15). The most vigorous effort was during the reign of Hezekiah (715-687 BC) whose concern was that Judah should not share the fate of the Kingdom of Samaria recently incorporated into the Assyrian empire. Here, too, cultic reform went hand in hand with political emancipation and included the important innovation of abolishing the high places (2 Kgs. 18: 3 – 8, 22); in which respect Hezekiah anticipated the aims of the reform party during Josiah's reign. Putting all this together, Deuteronomy can be explained as embodying the programme of the reform party which matured over a relatively long period of time and was redacted at the court of Josiah dominated by the traditionalist and anti-Assyrian faction.

In describing Josiah's reforms, the historian speaks only of the re-affirmation of the worship of Yahweh and the rejection of pagan or syncretist practices. In the light of the international situation, this emphasis on native tradition is understandable and has parallels in similar situations elsewhere. The Deuteronomic programme, however, goes beyond this by relating cultic fidelity to the task of creating a just society. Its utopian character is apparent in its abolition of poverty – 'there will be no poor among you' (15: 4) – and its overriding insistence on justice in every aspect of national life – 'justice, and only justice, you shall pursue' (16: 20). At the same time, it laid down precise dispositions in defence of the most disadvantaged classes of society including widows, fatherless, aliens, and the unemployed. It goes beyond the Covenant Code in its insistence on the remission of debts in the seventh year and adds appropriate measures to prevent evasion or abuse of the law (15: 1-11). Usury and abusive debt collection, which had contributed to driving many farmers off the land, are prohibited (23: 19-20; 24: 6, 10-13, 17), and there are provisions for the protection and, in some cases, the emancipation of slaves which go well beyond the measures in the Covenant Code (15: 12-18; 23: 15-16; 24: 7).

The Deuteronomic legislation reflects awareness of the fact that measures of this kind, however well-intentioned, are not likely to be effective so long as the institutional structures of the society remain immune to reform and regeneration. There are therefore stipulations concerning the conduct of local judges (16: 18-20), to which is added the innovation of a central judiciary and court of appeals referred to earlier (17: 8-13). There are also provisions governing the employment and support of clergy (18: 1-8) and, most significantly, a 'mirror for kings' which, in effect, sets up a constitutional monarchy (17: 14-20).

One of the most interesting features of the Deuteronomic programme is its concern to preserve a traditional agrarian way of life based on the rights of the free farmer. The ancient prohibition against removing boundary marks (19: 14), which occurs also in the instructions (e.g. Prov. 22: 28), was aimed at the abuse of enclosure denounced by the prophets (e.g. Mic. 2: 2). Concern for property, one's own and that of others, is even extended to birds' nests (22: 6-7). Enlightened provisions for release from military service (20: 5-9; 24: 5) were intended to alleviate a long-standing source of bitterness between the agrarian class and the monarchy. The priestly tithe is quite restricted (18: 1-8), and support of the national cult, another problem area, is to be proportionate to the individual's means (16: 6-7).

One of the most vigorous debates among Old Testament scholars, which has been going on for over a century, has to do with the author or authors of this programme. The high level of interest in this issue is understandable, since we are dealing with a text which marks the watershed between Israel as a nation state and Judaism as a religion based on law and worship. At one time it seemed well established that its origins were to be sought in the territory of the Northern Kingdom. Similarities with the so-called Elohist source in the Pentateuch (E), allegedly of northern provenance, and with the Ephraimite prophet Hosea, were adduced in evidence. The Elohist narrative strand has, however, proved to be rather elusive, and its northern origin difficult to establish with a comfortable degree of probability. Deuteronomy certainly reflects the language of Hosea at several points, but it also owes a debt to Judaean prophets. Hosea, moreover, shows little concern with the kind of social abuses which Deuteronomy combats.

Another line of enquiry has traced the distinctive character of the book, and especially its strong homiletic style, to Levites, again with special emphasis on northern Levites. But the problem here is that our principal sources, the Deuteronomic History and the pre-exilic prophets, never mention Levites as a class of minor clergy active during the monarchy. The only exception is the reference to the exclusion of Levites from employment in the state sanctuaries of the Northern Kingdom under Jeroboam (1 Kgs. 12: 31). The post-exilic Chronicler's description of Levites acting as instructors in Torah during the time of the monarchy reflects the situation obtaining in his own day and is clearly anachronistic. Deuteronomy itself refers to Levites as a distinct and subordinate clerical class only in one passage (27: 14) which belongs to the latest editorial stratum of the book. As for the homiletic style of the book, we have no evidence that it derives from levitical preaching. In fact, where the language of preaching is used in First Temple texts, it is referred not to Levites but to prophets (e.g. Am. 7: 16; Mic. 2: 6, 11; Ezek. 21: 1, 7).

Taking everything into account, including the many uncertainties, it is plausible to conclude that the Deuteronomic programme represents a deposit of religious and social reform which peaked shortly after the destruction of the Northern Kingdom (722 BC), was dormant during the long reign of Manasseh (687-642 BC), and achieved its greatest, if no less short-lived, success under Josiah. The most important single factor in this sporadic movement of reform was prophetic preaching. Here the operative distinction was not so much between northern and southern prophets as between provincial and metropolitan. Micah came not from Jerusalem but from a town called Moresheth in the Judaean foothills south-west of the capital. We know that he influenced the reforms of Hezekiah (see Jer. 26: 16-19), and there are numerous points of contact between his indictment of his contemporaries and the social legislation in Deuteronomy, e.g., removing landmarks, usury, unjust exploitation of debtors, falsifying weights and measures, and bribery. This leads us to suspect that the initial impetus to reform, generated by Micah and perhaps other prophets like him, came from outside Jerusalem and especially from the freehold farming class, religiously conservative and anti-Assyrian, which is known as 'the people of the land'. It was this class which put Josiah on the throne (2 Kgs. 21: 24) and retained its political influence down to the end of national independence (e.g. 2 Kgs. 25: 15).

Another aspect of Deuteronomy, one of particular interest for the theme of our study, is its scribal character. This is apparent in the insistence that the laws be studied, explained and taught (e.g. 1: 5; 4: 1, 10, 36; 5: 1) as a God-given discipline (4: 36; 8: 5; 11: 2) following which leads to wisdom (4: 6). Moses is teacher and scribe; as such, he not only enunciates the laws but provides motivation for their observance, e.g., in the refrain that runs through the book, 'that you may live long in the land which Yahweh your God is giving you'. Exhortations to take heed, to recall the experiences of the past, to acknowledge the truth of what is being said, give a character and tone to the book which inevitably call to mind the style of the sages in Proverbs and other sapiential compositions. There can be no doubt that in Deuteronomy the legal and sapiential traditions flow together.

An important result of the confluence of the two traditions is that the law can no longer be considered as a purely objective and extrinsic reality, much less as a necessary evil or an infringement on personal freedom necessary for the preservation of society. On the contrary, the 'sapientializing' of the law implies that it is to be internalized by an activity which unites learning and piety in the pursuit of a common purpose:

> You will seek Yahweh your God, and you will find him if you search after him with all your heart and with all your soul.
> (4: 29)

It is this *searching*, through study and observance of Torah, which will emerge with increasing clarity as the hallmark of early Judaism after the return from the exile.

It was suggested earlier that this scribal character of the book resulted from its status as an official document commissioned by the king. The royal scribe, attested from the time of the United Monarchy, was a high official with a wide range of responsibilities. During the reign of Josiah the royal scribe Shaphan supervised the repair of the temple and it was to him that the scroll found there was handed. It was also he who read it to the king and who was sent to consult with the prophetess Huldah as to what should be done about it (2 Kgs. 22: 3–20). This does not, of course, imply

67628

that he and his colleagues at the court were responsible for writing the book, as some have suggested. It seems much more likely that it was redacted by law scribes or 'handlers of the law' (Jer. 2: 8) who formed a specialized corps within the ranks of the temple clergy and were the ancestors of the Levitical scribes of the Second Temple period. This was, as we have seen, a new development, since specialized legal interpretation was called for only when there was an authoritative written law to be interpreted. Its importance for the future can hardly be exaggerated.

An important corollary is that the same class was responsible for the mature formulation of ideas about the covenant which we find in Deuteronomy. It is at this point that the political analogy, i.e., appeal to Assyrian vassal treaties, carries most weight. The book itself testifies to its character as a political manifesto, a declaration of independence from foreign control and a re-affirmation of national identity: a strong feeling for the land, emphasis on the holy war, Israel as Yahweh's possession, sin as an act of rebellion against 'the great, mighty and terrible God' (10: 17). While repudiating links with foreign 'principalities and powers', Deuteronomy re-affirms Israel's covenant bond with Yahweh as the source of its collective existence. The strength of this re-affirmation was such that, even though the bid for independence and the religious reforms themselves were short-lived, it could still provide inspiration for the new generation which returned to the land after the exile.

5

Law in Early Judaism: Temple Community and Sect

The Priestly source (P)

All critical scholars and most general readers of the Bible now recognize that the Pentateuch is the result of a long period of growth and development. In the previous chapter we looked at one aspect of this process which resulted in Deuteronomy and the closely related history corresponding to the Former Prophets (Joshua to Kings). We can be reasonably confident that these two compositions were complete by the early Persian period, i.e., the late sixth and early fifth centuries BC, when the descendants of those Judaeans who had been deported were able to return to the homeland.

The first four books of the Pentateuch, which tell the story from creation to the end of Israel's wandering in the wilderness, present problems of a more formidable nature several of which still await a solution. We shall be concerned with the laws contained in these books, but the point has been made more than once that these can be understood only in the narrative context in which they are presented. This context must therefore first be discussed if only in a brief and summary fashion. Most critical scholars believe that it is possible to trace a process by which two narrative strands, running more or less parallel and based on a common stock of traditional material, were transmitted separately in the Northern and Southern kingdoms. At some point, probably shortly before or after the fall of the Northern Kingdom in the late eighth century BC, they were conflated in Judah, resulting in one epic narrative of the nation's origins. This appears to have been a time of intense literary activity both in Israel and in neighbouring lands. The Assyrian kings, for example, were at that time assembling and editing ancient mythological and epic texts for their great library in Nineveh and, further afield, the Homeric poems were being written up in their present form.

Since the principal theme of the story of Israel's ancestors in Gen. 12–50 is the promise of nationhood and land, this basic epic narrative must have included the occupation of Canaan and therefore have constituted a Hexateuch rather than a Pentateuch (i.e., a six-book collection including Joshua). About the time of the Babylonian exile it was then re-edited to bring it into conformity with the needs and aspirations of those who had survived the disasters of the early sixth century BC. Since this re-editing is strongly marked by ritual and cultic concerns, it has been attributed to priests and is therefore known as the Priestly source (P).

With its highly distinctive style, fondness for genealogies and concern for exact chronology, P has proved to be the easiest of the narrative strands in the Pentateuch to identify. Problems still awaiting a satisfactory solution are its relation with the earlier narrative and its precise extent. All agree that it opens with the creation recital in Gen. 1: 1 − 2: 4 which highlights the seven-day liturgical week, the fixing of the religious calendar (on the fourth day, 1: 14), and sabbath (2: 2-3). There is no such firm consensus as to its ending. Some find it at the end of Deuteronomy where the death of Moses is described in typically priestly language:

Moses went up from the plains of Moab to Mount Nebo . . . which is opposite Jericho . . . Moses was a hundred and twenty years old when he died; his eye was not dim, nor his natural force abated. And the people of Israel wept for Moses in the plains of Moab thirty days; then the days of weeping and mourning for Moses were ended. And Joshua the son of Nun was full of the spirit of wisdom, for Moses had laid his hands upon him; so the people of Israel obeyed him, and did as Yahweh had commanded Moses. (34: 1, 7-9)

Others, however, believe that it continued on to the setting up of the wilderness sanctuary in Canaan and the partitioning of the land among the tribes:

> Then the whole congregation of the people of Israel assembled at Shiloh, and set up the tent of meeting there; the land lay subdued before them . . . These are the inheritances which Eleazar the priest and Joshua the son of Nun and the heads of the fathers' houses of the tribes of the people of Israel distributed by lot at Shiloh before Yahweh, at the door of the tent of meeting. So they finished dividing the land.
>
> (Jos. 18: 1; 19: 51)

If P did continue down to this point, as seems quite likely from the evidence of style and vocabulary, it could be seen to reflect the aspirations of the exilic generation for a return to the land and the re-establishment of worship as the first stage of a new dispensation.

The further and final stage by which we arrive at a Pentateuch rather than a Hexateuch is without doubt the most difficult and the most neglected in critical study. All we can do here is present a possible reconstruction in the barest outline. At some point Deuteronomy was incorporated into the basic narrative edited by the Priestly school. When this happened the decision was also made to conclude this narrative with the death of Moses and thus exclude the account of the conquest and settlement. This involved postponing the death of Moses which, as a careful reading will show, originally came at a certain point in the Priestly version of the wilderness wanderings (Num. 27: 12-23). The editor responsible for this adjustment, who stood in the same tradition as the Priestly school of the exilic period, simply added a date at the beginning of Deuteronomy (1: 3), thus bringing the entire book elegantly within the P chronology, and introduced an updated version of the commissioning of Joshua and death of Moses at the end (Deut. 32: 48-52; 34: 1, 7-9).

The general reader may be excused for being somewhat impatient with these hypothetical reconstructions, but the fact of the matter is that the stages by which the Pentateuch reached its present form correspond to different stages in the religious history of Israel and early Judaism. And, for our present purpose, it is possible to understand the development of the legal tradition only as an aspect of this literary prehistory. A people retains its vitality, even its identity, only at the price of continually re-thinking and re-appropriating its traditions in the light of new situations, especially when these situations are of a profoundly disorientating kind. That Torah was brought to an end with the death of Moses rather than with the conquest of the land, for example, corresponds to a very significant shift in the way post-exilic Judaism came to understand its own character and destiny. At an earlier stage, the different ways in which the Priestly source (P) edited or amplified the existing narrative tradition provide important clues to the adjustments and changes forced on the community as a result of political disaster and exile. The following examples may serve to illustrate the point:

(i) The addiction of P to genealogies can be explained by the need for continuity in an age of discontinuity and for legitimation with the emergence of a new order. The genealogy which interrupts the P version of Moses' commissioning (Ex. 6: 14–25), for example, traces the priestly lineage back to Aaron, elder brother of Moses, and through him to Levi, and thus established the temple priesthood of the early post-exilic period on a firm basis of antiquity.

(ii) The greatly enhanced role of Aaron in the same P version of the commissioning (Ex. 6: 2 – 7: 7; cf. the earlier version, 3: 1 – 6: 1) reflects the dominant position won by the priesthood after the return from exile and re-establishment of worship in Jerusalem. To a considerable extent, the priesthood took over the functions of the monarchy after the latter had disappeared from history.

(iii) The need to guard against the dangers of assimilation, a major preoccupation during the exile and after the return to the land, is reflected in the P version of the Jacob saga. It is the priestly editor who explains Jacob's flight to Mesopotamia by the need to avoid marriage with a Canaanite woman and holds up Esau's marriage with Hittite women as an example of the deplorable effects of such unions (Gen. 26: 34-5; 27: 46 – 28: 5). In general, P presents Jacob as the prototype of those Jews who went into exile in Mesopotamia, remained faithful there, and returned to claim their inheritance.

(iv) The high points of the P narrative are the creation of the world, with its obvious cultic allusions referred to above (Gen. 1: 1 – 2: 4), the setting up of the sanctuary and inauguration of worship in the wilderness (Ex. 25-31; 35-40) and (according to our reconstruction presented above) the final coming to rest of the same sanctuary in the promised land (Jos. 18: 1; 19: 51). This corresponds to a re-interpretation of the history as the progressive revelation of a cultic order by means of which God has chosen to be present to his people. And, in keeping with this re-interpretation, the promise of land and nationhood is amplified with the promise of divine presence: I will be your God, I will be with you.

(v) The P narrative has also modified the older understanding of covenant. Only in P does God make a covenant with Noah, and therefore with mankind in the archaic period before Israel came into existence (Gen. 9: 8-17). At a later point, the covenant with the ancestors is modified to introduce the institution of circumcision (Gen. 17: 1-21). These solemn agreements with the nations and with Israel are perpetually binding, irreversible and therefore not in need of renewal. Thereafter God *remembers* his covenant with the ancestors whenever his people call on him, whether in exile in Egypt (Ex. 2: 24) or elsewhere (Lev. 26: 42, 45). In keeping with this chronological shift, the P strand of the Sinai story focusses only on the establishment of the cult, singling out the institution of sabbath as a sign of creation and a perpetual covenant (Ex. 31: 12-17). Covenant implies, for the nations, the obligation to respect life (Gen. 9: 4-6) and additionally, for Israel, circumcision and sabbath observance. It is these institutions, laid down at the beginning of its history, which give Israel its peculiar character as willed by God.

It was along these lines, then, that history was reinterpreted by the Priestly school to meet the critical situation of the sixth century BC and, at the same time, maintain the essential link with the past. With the gradual return to the homeland after the Persian conquest of Babylon (539 BC), Judah took shape as one of several provinces in a satrapy of the Persian empire. Like some of the Greek city states in Ionia, its status was determined by its temple which served not only as a place of prayer and sacrifice but as the administrative and financial centre of the province. The civic status of the individual, even his title to property, depended on participation in and support of temple worship. Hence the great power of the priesthood in both the religious and the political sphere, backed as it was by the central government which subsidized the cult (cf. Ezra 6: 4, 8) and enforced the observance of local laws (cf. Ezra 7: 25f.).

This last point may serve as a reminder that the laws of the Pentateuch, or such of them as were in force at that time, formed in effect the civic constitution of the province of Judah. We know that it was Persian policy to insist on the promulgation and observance of such local laws, including laws which regulated worship. As early as the reign of Cyrus we hear complaints of royal commissioners that the priests in Babylon were negligent in carrying out the cult of Marduk, god of that city. A later king, Darius, ordered a codification of Egyptian laws and, later still, a letter written by the satrap of Egypt ordered the Jewish military colony at Elephantine (Assuan) on the Upper Nile to celebrate the feast of Unleavened Bread in the traditional manner. We have therefore no reason to doubt the report that another Persian king sent Ezra as a kind of royal commissioner to Jerusalem to see that 'the law of the God of heaven' was enforced among Jews in that satrapy (Ezra 7: 11-26). In short, all the indications are that the Persian period must have been decisive for the codification of the laws in the Pentateuch.

Cultic and ritual laws

From the very earliest times in Israel the correct performance of the cult was an essential aspect of public order and wellbeing. To participate in public worship was to share in the praise and adoration of God carried on unceasingly in the heavenly world and, in doing so, to fulfil the goal of existence. We recall how Isaiah received his prophetic commission through a vision in which he was admitted to this heavenly liturgy and heard the seraphim singing the divine praise (Isa. 6: 1-13). The same idea appears here and there in the Psalms, and when God answered Job out of the whirlwind he spoke of the dedication liturgy accompanying the creation of the world conceived as a vast temple:

Where were you when I laid the foundations of the earth?
  Tell me, if you have understanding.
Who determined its measurements – surely you know!
  Or who stretched the line upon it?
On what were its bases sunk, or who laid its cornerstone,
  when the morning stars sang together,
  and all the sons of God shouted for joy?   (Job 38: 4–7)

The importance of the liturgical calendar, as determining the course of sacred time, is indicated by its origins in the first week of creation (Gen. 1: 14). Similar considerations operated on the spatial axis, since the sanctuary was constructed according to heavenly specifications dictated by God himself (Ex. 25: 9, 40; 26: 30). To share in worship then, according to this perspective, was to participate to the fullest extent in reality and to live according to a divinely willed order.

It follows from this world view that the purpose of the many cultic acts carried out in the temple was to maintain and, where necessary, re-establish this divine order. Sin was understood as a disturbance of that order, even when committed by inadvertence. The sacrificial cult was in fact designed primarily, if not exclusively, to remove the effects of inadvertent sin. For deliberate sinful acts, those committed 'with a high hand' (Num. 15: 30–1), there could be no remission through the cult. In rejecting the law, the sinner rejected its author, thereby putting himself outside the community and beyond the reach of the redemptive possibilities available within it.

Whatever our own views may be, it is important for us to understand the perspective which informs the ritual laws in the Pentateuch. To be in a sinful state is not just a matter of ethics as we understand it. It is to be in a wrong relationship to an order which is built into the fabric of a world created by God. Hence the concern for bodily states, the food one eats, physical contacts, and the like. Holiness is not just a matter of internal states and acts. It must also encompass the material world, and therefore also the body as that part of the world for which each one is more directly responsible.

The bulk of the cultic and ritual law is in Leviticus and Numbers, and is presented as given by Yahweh from the sanctuary immediately after its construction at Sinai. This no doubt corresponds to one of the most important functions of the temple personnel in the post-exilic period. While much of this sanctuary law is undoubtedly ancient, we should probably think of a major redaction taking place shortly before or shortly after the restoration of temple worship in the early Persian period, with much supplementary material added at intervals thereafter. The setting for the giving of these laws is provided by the Priestly narrative. P marks the point of Israel's arrival at and departure from Sinai (Ex. 19: 1; Num. 10: 11-28), but otherwise concentrates exclusively on the establishment of the cult. Moses encountered the mysterious presence of God — referred to as 'the Glory' — on the mountain, received the detailed specifications for the wilderness sanctuary and its appointments (25-31), and saw to their execution (35-40). The only legal enactment mentioned here is the sabbath rest, enjoined under pain of death. It is to be a sign of creation and, like circumcision, a perpetual covenant (Ex. 31: 12-17).

This last point gives us a clue to the relation between narrative and law in the Priestly source. In some episodes the narrative is rewritten to bring it into conformity with cultic or ritual law. According to P, for example, the Israelites in the wilderness collected a double quantity of manna on the sixth day so as to avoid violating the sabbath law (Ex. 16: 5, 22-30). The divine will is progressively revealed in specific enactments at different points in the history. The prohibition against eating meat with the blood in it is first heard after the flood and is therefore meant to be universally binding (Gen. 9: 4-6). The covenant with Abraham introduces the rite of circumcision, and its immediate execution therefore signifies the official establishment of Israel as a people apart (Gen. 17: 9-27). The exodus from Egypt provides the appropriate occasion for introducing the Passover ritual (Ex. 12: 1-20). A later stipulation, that the corpse-contaminated person celebrate it a month later apart from the community (Num. 9: 1-14), provides an interesting example of development. The sabbath, finally, is given at Sinai though its observance is anticipated in the wilderness.

Leviticus, known in Jewish tradition as 'the law of the priests', contains several collections of cultic and ritual law which were originally distinct. Lev. 1-7 is one of these, dealing with the different kinds of sacrifice and the economically important matter of allocating sacrificial material. That it was an originally independent manual is apparent from the fact that Lev. 8-10 continue the Priestly Sinai narrative. For these chapters treat of the ordination of Aaron and his sons as priests, the inauguration of their priesthood, and the elimination of the two older sons, Nadab and Abihu, for failure to observe the exact ritual. This last episode, incidentally, is one of several in P which reflect the struggle for power among priestly families which left the Zadokites firmly in control. Another collection, Lev. 11-15, deals with ritual impurity and bodily emissions. It is followed by the ritual for the Day of Atonement (Yom Kippur) in Lev. 16 which may be of quite late date since the great fast and penitential rite convoked by Ezra followed different rules (Neh. 9: 1). The most important collection, however, is the one known to modern scholarship as the Holiness Code (H), widely thought to be a separate text covering various aspects of the demand for holiness (Lev. 17-26).

A glance at the contents of Lev. 17-26 will show that it is by no means as orderly and homogeneous as the title 'Holiness Code' might lead one to think. Like the Deuteronomic law, it opens with a prohibition of sacrificing outside the central sanctuary, followed by a prohibition of eating meat with the blood in it. In both cases reasons are given for the prohibition (Lev. 17). The next chapter (Lev. 18) gives the impression of being a separate manual containing a series of twelve types of forbidden sexual relations most of which have to do with incest. These are followed by other offences which defile the land: sexual relations with a woman during her period, adultery, the sacrifice of children (the so-called *molek* sacrifices attested among the Phoenicians and Carthaginians), homosexuality and bestiality. The section begins and ends with divine address presenting these laws as safeguarding the life and character of Israel as it prepares to live in its own land.

So far there has been no mention of holiness. The demand that the people be holy in conformity with the holiness of their God occurs for the first time at the beginning and end of the next section (Lev. 19-20):

You shall be holy; for I, Yahweh your God, am holy.   (19: 2)

I am Yahweh your God who have separated you from the peoples. You shall therefore make a distinction between the clean beast and the unclean, and between the unclean bird and the clean . . . You shall be holy to me; for I Yahweh am holy, and have separated you from the peoples, that you should be mine.   (20: 24-6)

The stipulations in this section are both ethical and ritual, though it should be observed that this distinction was unknown to the redactors of the laws and those to whom they were addressed. Leaving aside Lev. 19: 5-9, which is an appendix to the rules governing sacrifice in Lev. 3, we find here most of the stipulations of the decalogue together with laws against necromancy (black magic) and a variety of pagan practices, some of them associated with the cult of the dead. Somewhat surprisingly, however, these are juxtaposed with dispositions in favour of the poor and disadvantaged in society, e.g., gleaning rights, the prompt payment of wages, and care for the deaf, blind, and aged.

As in the Deuteronomic legislation, with which this section has much in common, one has the impression that these measures are only examples of what is involved in creating and maintaining a just society. They are summarized in the command to love and not to hate:

You shall not hate your brother in your heart, but you shall reason with your neighbour, lest you bear sin because of him. You shall not take vengeance or bear any grudge against the sons of your own people, but you shall love your neighbour as yourself: I am Yahweh.   (19: 17-18)

While, in the context, 'neighbour' means fellow-Jew, it should be noted that the obligation also covers resident aliens:

When a stranger sojourns with you in your land, you shall not do him wrong. The stranger who sojourns with you shall be to you as the native among you, and you shall love him as yourself; for you were strangers in the land of Egypt. I am Yahweh your God.
(19: 33-4)

Following prophetic precedent, Jesus coupled this command with the Shema ('Hear, O Israel': Deut. 6: 4ff.) as a summary of the entire Torah (Mt. 22: 34-40).

The last part of this section (Lev. 20) contains, for the most part, the penalties attaching to violations of the 'sexual dodecalogue'; i.e., the twelve-unit series, Lev. 18. Its conclusion, quoted above, suggests that Lev. 19-20 is a self-contained unit which could more properly be called the Holiness Code than the larger composition to which that title is generally applied. The following chapters contain rules more specifically addressed to the priesthood (Lev. 21-2), a liturgical calendar (Lev. 23), and various stipulations concerning worship, the sabbatical year and the jubilee year (Lev. 24-5). As in Deuteronomy, the laws are rounded off with blessings and curses. These clearly reflect the exilic situation when Israel's God will remember his covenant with the ancestors (26: 40-2). It is also stated that the God whose will finds expression in the laws is also the God who sets free:

> I am Yahweh your God who brought you forth out of the land of Egypt, that you should not be their slaves; and I have broken the bars of your yoke and made you walk erect.   (26: 13)

In Leviticus and Numbers the ideal of holiness comes to expression in these and similar laws and, more generally, in the description of Israel in its wanderings through the desert to the promised land. Given the assumptions on which secular life is based, it is not easy for us today to grasp what holiness meant to the authors of these texts. It is clearly not restricted to the moral life as this is generally understood. In the Holiness Code it connotes an attempt to embody in the life of the individual and the community the character of a God who was totally other, apart from the world. Translated into principles of conduct, this imitation of God implied not only a high ethical ideal but a distinctive way of life which set the community apart from the surrounding cultures. Whatever the remote origin of rules governing food taboos and ritual defilement, which are not confined to ancient Israel and Judaism, it is more important to understand how they functioned as defining and maintaining this distinctive character.

To take an obvious example: the great vigilance concerning the sexual function, apparent in the Holiness Code, has to be seen as a reaction to the sacralization of sexuality in Canaanite fertility cults, with their 'holy ones' (cultic prostitutes, male and female) and orgiastic rites. During and after the exile, the purity laws acted as a powerful counter-force to the tendency towards assimilation. With the growth of the diaspora, demographic expansion and the adherence of increasing numbers of Gentiles to the Jewish faith, this tendency was bound to get stronger. On the other hand, it was also inevitable that, as Judaism became a worldwide faith, criticism would be levelled at these highly distinctive features which by then had achieved confessional status. This, however, belongs to a later stage of the history.

Law and order in the Chronicler's work

By the time of the Babylonian exile there were two substantial historical works in existence: the national epic edited by the Priestly school and the Deuteronomic History. To these we must now add a third: 1 and 2 Chronicles with Ezra and Nehemiah which, taken together, cover a vast sweep from creation to the mission of Nehemiah in the fifth century BC. This work drew on the earlier histories by using the Priestly genealogies to bridge the gap between creation and the monarchy and, from that point, by following more or less the Deuteronomic History. Its relationship to these earlier works is not, however, entirely clear. It may have been intended to supplant them but, if so, it appears that they were too firmly established for this to be possible. Another debated issue is the process by which the Chronicler's history reached its final form as we have it. That there were earlier drafts seems well established. That it drew on a somewhat different version of the history from the one now contained in the books of Samuel and Kings is at least possible. Some have found confirmation for this hypothesis in certain manuscript fragments of Samuel discovered in the fourth Qumran cave which are closer to Chronicles than to our Hebrew text of Samuel. For our present purpose the issue need not be pursued further.

The final version of the history, whatever its previous stages, cannot be dated with certainty. It must be later than the last events recorded in it, and these take us to the late fifth or early fourth century BC, depending on the dating of Ezra's mission. The absence of any allusion to the end of Persian rule and the author's sympathetic attitude to Persian rulers suggest a date prior to the conquest of Alexander in 332 BC. But this is only an educated guess, and would not in any case preclude later additions, e.g., some of the genealogies and the Memoirs of Nehemiah.

To come to the point which concerns us in this chapter, the Chronicler gives pride of place to 'the law of Moses' which he takes to be a law available in writing from the beginning. The frequent allusions which he makes to this law do not, however, necessarily point to the Pentateuch as we have it today. In dealing with legal matters he refers sometimes to Deuteronomy, sometimes to ritual laws in Leviticus and Numbers, and sometimes to enactments which either differ in some respect from Pentateuchal law or are not in the Pentateuch at all.

At one point he presents what purports to be a letter from the Persian king Artaxerxes — the context would naturally suggest Artaxerxes I (464–425 BC) — authorizing Ezra, a priest and scribe, to see that 'the law of the God of heaven' was known, understood, and observed among the Jews living in the Trans-Euphrates satrapy of the Persian empire (Ezra 7: 11-26). The same law book was subsequently read by Ezra and explained by Levites at a great open air convocation in Jerusalem (Neh. 8-9). In later Jewish tradition, represented by 1 Esdras and the Talmud, Ezra came to be regarded as a figure of heroic proportions, a second Moses who restored the Pentateuch after it had been destroyed by the Babylonians. Historically, however, Ezra's law book cannot be simply equated with the Pentateuch, though it may have represented an important stage in the formation of Pentateuchal legislation.

In dealing with the related concepts of law and covenant the Chronicler is remarkably innovative. His historical narrative omits entirely the history of the period prior to the monarchy, and thus also the giving of the law at Sinai. It begins instead with the death of Saul and the accession of David. One consequence is that great prominence is given to the covenant with David (1 Chr. 17, based on

2 Sam. 7), the periodic renewal of which punctuates the history of the monarchy. Needless to say, the author does not eliminate or discount the Mosaic covenant but he does follow the Priestly source in de-emphasizing it, probably with the idea that the Davidic covenant includes and subsumes the Mosaic. This shift of emphasis, which represents a surprising break with tradition, had the important effect of endowing royal decrees with divine authority. It could even serve to legitimate the measures taken by Ezra and Nehemiah, since both were emissaries of the Persian monarchy which was juridically, if temporarily, the successor to the Davidic dynasty.

A synoptic reading of the two versions of the Davidic covenant revealed by the prophet Nathan (2 Sam. 7 and 1 Chr. 17) will also show how the Chronicler, by introducing small changes into the text, has linked the covenant firmly with the building of the temple and the cult to be carried on in it. The shift is especially clear in the final word of promise:

> Your house and your kingdom shall be made sure for ever before me. (2 Sam. 7: 16)

> I will confirm him in my house and in my kingdom for ever. (1 Chr. 17: 14)

Here there is a very definite shift of emphasis from dynasty to temple; all the more remarkable, in that the earlier version stressed the divine promise of a house (meaning dynasty) over against the human initiative of building a house (meaning temple). The Chronicler's point is demonstrated on a massive scale in his treatment of David's reign which occupies about one fifth of the entire history (1 Chr. 11-29). The events emphasized are: the bringing of the ark of the covenant to Jerusalem where it was attended by Levites, the elaborate preparations made by David for the building of the temple, the establishment of the priests in their twenty-four courses (an arrangement unknown to the Pentateuch) and of the Levites, liturgical musicians, and others in their several divisions and guilds. For the Chronicler, therefore, David's chief claim to fame was not as warrior and founder of a dynasty but as the one who laid the foundations for temple worship. It is further implied that the dynastic promise was fulfilled primarily through the establishment of the cult which it was the duty of his successors to maintain and, where necessary, restore to its original purity.

For the Chronicler the temple is the centre and focus of national life and the temple service the guarantee of order and wellbeing. So important is it that he does not hesitate to amend the history to bring it into line with correct liturgical practice. Since, according to law, only Levites could attend the ark, it had to be they who brought it up to Jerusalem during David's reign and ministered to it in its temporary resting place (1 Chr. 15-16). Since the king's sons could not be priests, as they are said to be at 2 Sam. 8: 18, they had to become chief officials instead (1 Chr. 18: 17). Levitical musicians had to play an important part in the dedication of Solomon's temple (2 Chr. 5: 11-13), and so on. In these and other respects the Chronicler reads his own situation back into the time of the monarchy. A further example, noted earlier, is his account of Levites going from city to city during the reign of Jehoshaphat instructing the people in Torah with the help of a law book which they took with them (2 Chr. 17: 7-9).

Unlike the Priestly source, the Chronicler understood covenant to be a public act involving king and people which must be repeated at intervals, and especially after one of the rather frequent intervals of religious infidelity. The pattern was set during the reign of Asa, one of the early Judaean kings: a great assembly during which the people sacrificed, accepted the covenant with a binding oath, and carried out a purification of the cult and of religious life in general (2 Chr. 14: 3-5; 15: 9-15). The covenant and reform initiated by the priest Jehoiada on behalf of the young king Joash followed the same pattern (23: 1-21). After the apostasy of Ahaz, an even more basic reform was carried out under Hezekiah whose renewal of the covenant was concluded with the celebration of Passover in Jerusalem (29-31). During the reforms of Josiah yet another factor was introduced, i.e., the public reading of the law book recently discovered in the temple (34). With this public reading the pattern of public assemblies in the Chronicler's own time was complete.

We have already noted the importance which the Chronicler gives to the mission of Ezra as emissary of the Persian central government. Alarmed at the number of people in the Jerusalem community who had married foreign wives, Ezra convoked a plenary gathering to make a covenant sealed with an oath to remedy the matter once and for all. The narrative ends on a realistic note with the information that the meeting was rained off and the issue, so to speak, sent to committee (Ezra 10). Neh. 9–10 also records a plenary assembly at which the law was read, sins were confessed, and a written document drawn up and signed. By means of this solemn and official act the signatories bound themselves to observe the law, avoid 'mixed marriages', keep the law of sabbath and sabbatical year in all strictness, and contribute to the upkeep of temple worship. While the narrative implies that the entire Judaean community took part in this assembly, it seems more likely that this *written* covenant (9: 38) involved a more limited group which supported the reforms. The impression given is almost of a sectarian gathering, an anticipation of the solemn covenanting of the Qumran community.

For the Chronicler, at any rate, the decisive factor in the way the community understood itself and ordered its life was the existence of a *written* law. Assuming consistency in his reading of the history, this law book would be the one which was rediscovered during the reign of Josiah (2 Chr. 34). Since it was available and in use during the reign of Jehoshaphat more than two centuries earlier (2 Chr. 17: 7–9), he presumably wishes us to believe that it was forgotten or lost during the interval between Jehoshaphat and Josiah, perhaps during the dark days of Manasseh in the first half of the seventh century BC. There can be no doubt that the book in question is our Deuteronomy, in whatever form it was known to the Chronicler. In fact, the only time he cites it — following his source — the quotation is from the Deuteronomic law (2 Chr. 25: 4; cf. Deut. 24: 16). It was also, presumably, on the basis of the same law book that the diaspora community, newly returned from Babylon, restored religious life in the homeland (Ezra 3: 2; 6: 18). There are indications, however, that he was also familiar with some at least of the cultic and ritual laws in Leviticus and Numbers. The feast of Tabernacles at the time of Ezra, for example, follows the calendric law in Leviticus rather than Deuteronomy (Neh. 8: 14–18). We observe here how the gradual development towards a comprehensive Torah, the

Pentateuch as we have it, followed the evolving and expanding need for normative order in the post-exilic community.

It is also noteworthy that this law book is now the object of study and interpretation, the results of which are to be made available to the entire community. While the paradigm is Ezra, the priest and scribe, who 'had set his heart to study the law of Yahweh, and to do it, and to teach his statutes and ordinances in Israel' (Ezra 7: 10), the task of day to day instruction fell to the Levites. At the great assembly convened by Ezra, for the Chronicler an event of historic importance, the Levites not only helped Ezra read the law publicly but provided a running commentary:

> The Levites helped the people to understand the law, while the people remained in their places. And they read from the book, from the law of God, clearly; and they gave the sense, so that the people understood the reading. (Neh. 8: 7-8)

It is unfortunate that the meaning of the key words 'clearly' and 'gave the sense' is far from clear. Some have thought to find here the origin of the practice by which the Hebrew text was provided with a targum or paraphrase in the language of the people. This would assume that, by the time of Ezra's mission, or at least by the time of writing, the population in Jerusalem not only spoke Aramaic but no longer understood Hebrew. Since this is more than we know, it is safer to assume that what the Levites did was provide exposition of the law. This activity, known as *midrash halakah*, i.e., the discussion and exposition of law with the purpose of establishing legal principles and handing down legal decisions, has remained one of the central characteristics of Jewish intellectual and religious life.

A final point calls for consideration. According to the perspective of this work, the law defines the community and determines who is and is not to belong to it. It would therefore be appropriate to ask what exactly is the community with which the author identifies. The genealogies in the first part of the work (1 Chr. 1-9) provide an initial clue with their progressive narrowing down from all mankind to the descendants of Abraham, then to Judah and the line of David carried down to the time of writing. In retelling the history of the monarchy he omits almost all mention of the Northern Kingdom and represents the establishment of a separate cult at Bethel and Dan as a lapse into paganism, a worship of demons and satyrs who are 'no gods' (2 Chr. 13: 9). Thus the northern tribes and their descendants, the inhabitants of Samaria, are no longer part of the 'Israel of God'. The true Israel continued in Judah under Hezekiah, constituting the 'remnant' which had escaped the Assyrian yoke and which came together in Jerusalem to celebrate a great Passover (2 Chr. 30). The parallelism with the other 'remnant' which returned from the Babylonian exile and celebrated Passover at the dedication of the temple is inescapable (Ezra 6: 19–22). It points to the author's conviction that it is through this group which went into exile, answered the call to return, rebuilt the temple and re-established its worship unaided by the local population, that the legitimate line of descent is carried on. For the Chronicler, then, the true Israel is the diaspora-group (Ezra 4: 1 etc.), the 'holy race' (Ezra 9: 2), which maintained and reinforced its distinctive character after the return, and especially after the reforms of Ezra and Nehemiah.

Historical objectivity requires us to add that this view of the Chronicler is polemical and one-sided. The many other Jews in the homeland and elsewhere who did not belong to this 'holy race' would no doubt have put it differently, but their opinions have not been allowed to survive. It has already been hinted that this kind of situation, with one group claiming to be the true Israel over against others, contains the seeds of sectarianism, even though sects do not clearly emerge until later in the Second Temple period. We are reminded that the Chronicler's account of social and religious order and his attempt at constructing a community model and ideal present only one of several possibilities, but one which would have a profound influence on later developments.

Law and legal exposition in the sects

In his account of the activity of Ezra and Nehemiah, the Chronicler assumes the existence of an élite group, composed of those who had returned from the Babylonian diaspora, which consciously set itself apart from other Jews in the land of Israel. By means of a special covenant and oath this group dedicated itself to a strict interpretation of the law as they understood it, with special reference to inter-marriage, sabbath, and the upkeep of the temple. We noted that the making of such covenants, with the precise stipulations and even the names of the signatories in writing, marks a stage in the development which would lead to sectarianism, precisely by empha-sizing the contractual basis for membership in the community. This will help to explain why such groups, when they do emerge, refer to themselves as 'the holy covenant', 'the sons of the covenant', 'the new covenant', and the like.

It was also noted how the Chronicler attests to the growing importance of legal exposition. Once we have passed to a written law as the decisive instrument of public order, those who were professionally responsible for its interpretation were bound to exercize increasing influence. The Chronicler restricts this task largely if not exclusively to Levites. Eventually, it would be shared by laymen, a shift which no doubt owes a considerable debt to the Pharisees. (We recall the frequent allusion in the gospels to 'scribes and Pharisees'.) Writing in the early second century BC, Ben Sira attests that the scribe was first and foremost a legal scholar with the responsibility of teaching others:

> On the other hand he who devotes himself
>   to the study of the law of the Most High
> will seek out the wisdom of all the ancients,
>   and will be concerned with prophecies . . .
> He will reveal instruction in his teaching,
>   and will glory in the law of Yahweh's covenant.
>   (Ecclus. 39: 1, 8)

By that time the teaching in question was carried on in schools, perhaps already associated with synagogues:

> Draw near to me, you who are untaught,
>   and lodge in my school.   (51: 23)

Despite the gaps in our knowledge of the period, it is reasonable to surmise that some of the scholarship of that time has survived in the great corpus of legal material codified in the Mishnah almost four centuries later. It is a fact, at any rate, that the earliest rabbinic sages to whom sayings are attributed in the Mishnah lived no more than a generation or so after the time of Ben Sira.

While this was going on, the sects were beginning to develop their own brand of legal interpretation. The little that we know about them indicates a remarkable variety with respect both to the claims underlying the process and the conclusions reached. It is important to emphasize this variety, since in Judaism, as also in Christianity, the uniformity achieved or imposed by the religious orthodoxy which eventually arose has tended to dominate our understanding of the past.

The conquests of Alexander placed Palestinian Jews under the rule of kings and courts which were Greek in language and culture: first, the Ptolemies in the third century who ruled from Alexandria in Egypt; then the Seleucids in Antioch in Syria who followed them. After more than half a century of rule, the latter were obliged to grant a measure of independence to Judaea in 142 BC. The dominance of the Greek way of life, with its strong drive to cultural homogeneity, resulted inevitably in the erosion of religious traditions and local cults all over the vast empire carved out by Alexander. Since Greek religion was intimately part of civic life, with sacrifices accompanying every kind of public act, it was practically impossible for those Jews living in the cities to aspire to the professions or to public office without in some way compromising their faith.

In the course of time such typically Greek institutions as the theatre, ephebeion (youth centre) and gymnasium were established in Jerusalem itself. Schools embodying the humanistic ideals of Greek education (*paideia*) inevitably exerted a considerable attraction. One has only to read Qoheleth who (as we saw earlier, pp. 63-9) is conversant with philosophical currents of the Ptolemaic age and never mentions Torah. The situation was, in some respects, similar to that in which European Jews found themselves during the Enlightenment. The available options can easily be detailed. One could embrace the new world view and bring the laws into conformity with it; one could reject it out of hand, insisting on a more rigorous interpretation of the laws; or, the course no doubt taken by most, one could make whatever pragmatic accommodations seemed to be called for without feeling obliged to take a clear stand.

This last option became more difficult to maintain after the accession of the Seleucid king Antiochus IV Epiphanes in 175 BC. At first favourable to the large Jewish population in his kingdom, Antiochus was soon driven by his desperate need for funds to impose heavy taxation and even plunder the temple treasury. By 167 BC matters came to a head with a royal decree of unification which, in effect, proscribed the Jewish religion. This was followed by the establishment of the cult of Zeus, patron god of the dynasty, in the Jerusalem temple. This first 'final solution of the Jewish problem' provoked its reaction in armed rebellion and guerilla warfare which, under the leadership of the Maccabee family, led to the re-occupation of Jerusalem (with the exception of the citadel), the cleansing of the temple and, eventually, a considerable measure of independence.

While this persecution was only too real, it is important to note that the chain of events leading to it began with a crisis internal to the Jewish community. We get hints of it in Ben Sira, writing a few years before the accession of Antiochus, where he condemns hypocrites who 'stumble over the law' (Ecclus. 32: 15) and an ungodly people who have forsaken it (41: 8). In the historical context this would refer to those who were accommodating the law to contemporary culture inspired by Greek ideals. Our principal source for the Antiochaean crisis, 1 Maccabees written about 100 BC, is quite explicit on this point:

> In those days [i.e. following the accession of Antiochus] lawless men came forth from Israel, and misled many, saying, 'Let us go and make a covenant with the Gentiles round about us, for since we separated from them many evils have come upon us.' This proposal pleased them, and some of the people eagerly went to the king. He authorized them to observe the ordinances of the Gentiles. So they built a gymnasium in Jerusalem, according to Gentile custom, and removed the marks of circumcision, and abandoned the holy covenant. They joined with the Gentiles and sold themselves to do evil. (1: 11–15)

It is natural that the author, writing as an apologist for the Maccabees and the Hasmonaean principate which they founded, should represent these opponents as simply abandoning Judaism for a Gentile life-style. More probably, however, these 'Hellenizers', led by priestly families including that of the high priest himself, had evolved their own understanding of the law so as to allow for a large area of accommodation to contemporary Greek culture. Some may have gone as far as to deny the divine origin of the Mosaic law, putting it on the same footing as other codes, those of Lycurgus and Solon, for example. Others would have been content to argue that certain more specifically Jewish features of the law — circumcision, sabbath rest, food taboos — were later accretions which should be abandoned as mere superstition. They could even have found arguments for accepting or at least tolerating the worship of Zeus. From the earliest days of the settlement in the land Yahweh had been seen by some to be an alternative embodiment of one of the gods of Canaan. After all, had not Abraham sworn to Melchizedek by Yahweh-El Elyon (Gen. 14: 22)?

Our principal source describes the conservative reaction to these measures and the persecution to which they led:

> Many in Israel stood firm and were resolved in their hearts not to eat unclean food. They chose to die rather than to be defiled by food or to profane the holy covenant; and they did die. And very great wrath came upon Israel. (1 Macc. 1: 62-3)

There were certainly more important things in Torah than the food laws but these, together with circumcision and sabbath, had been elevated to confessional status. 2 Maccabees, based on a five-volume history by Jason of Cyrene written in the first century BC, gives a more detailed account of these first Jewish martyrdoms: women hurled from the city walls for circumcising their children, others burnt alive for secretly observing sabbath, an aged scribe tortured to death for refusing to eat pork (6: 7-31). For the author of 1 Maccabees, the first organized resistance came from the country priest Mattathias and his sons (2: 1-28) who are described as fighting for the sanctuary and the law (14: 29). But he also speaks of 'many who were seeking righteousness and justice' who retired with their families into the Judaean wilderness and who, when confronted by the Seleucid forces on the sabbath, refused to fight and were promptly slaughtered (2: 29-38). Their sacrifice, which was prompted by fidelity to the law and not by pacifism, led to an important modification of the sabbath law permitting those attacked on the sabbath to resist (2: 39-41).

The same author goes on to mention another group called Asidaeans (corresponding to the Hebrew *hasidim*, meaning the devout or the faithful ones) who joined forces with Mattathias and his sons. They are described as a 'company' (literally 'synagogue'), warriors who offered themselves willingly for the law, opponents of the renegades or Hellenizers whom they attacked without mercy (2: 42-4). They may be the same as the 'assembly of the faithful' who fought alongside Judas Maccabee at the battle of Beth-horon (3: 13). We meet them again a little later together with a company of scribes negotiating terms of peace with the Seleucid general Bacchides and the newly appointed high priest Alcimus (Yakim), an incident which ended with the latter treacherously slaughtering sixty of their number (7: 12-18).

From these allusions we may deduce that these Asidaeans formed an identifiable group or association committed to the strict observance of the law and counting among their number those whose task was to interpret it. Since they were prepared to seek terms once the anti-Jewish edict had been repealed (6: 58-9), their stake in the struggle was clearly quite different from that of the Maccabees. They must also have attached great importance to the legitimacy of the high priestly office since they were led to negotiate by the appointment of one who, though no better than his predecessors, was at least of genuine Aaronite descent (7: 14).

This last point is important for understanding the sequence of events which led to the emergence of sects in the last two and a half centuries of the Second Temple. After the accession of Antiochus IV, the high priest Onias III was deposed and his place taken by Jason (Jesus) his brother who paid the new king handsomely for the favour. Not long afterwards, however, Jason was outbid by a certain Menelaus (Menahem), an even more enthusiastic devotee of the Greek way of life. More ominously, he was not even of legitimate Aaronite-Zadokite stock as required by the law. Alcimus, his successor, was at least an Aaronite and thus could command some measure of tolerance. By that time, however, a fatal precedent had been set whereby the high priesthood was filled by the Gentile ruler, generally on payment of a substantial bribe. The way was therefore prepared for Jonathan, brother and successor of Judas, to accept the offer from Alexander Balas, usurper of the Seleucid throne, and for his successor Simon to be confirmed in the office:

> The Jews and their priests decided that Simon should be their leader and high priest for ever, until a trustworthy prophet should arise. (1 Macc. 14: 41)

From what we have learned of the Asidaeans (Hasidim), we must conclude that they would have rejected this move out of hand. This, if anything, was the decisive issue leading to schism and the formation of sects in the strict sense of the term.

Several scholars have identified either Jonathan or Simon with the Wicked Priest of the Qumran scrolls who opposed the Teacher of Righteousness, founder and leader of the sect. It was, at any rate, on this crucial point of the legitimacy of the high priesthood that the Qumran sect, and possibly others, distanced themselves from the temple personnel and its services.

Internal evidence suggests that, in its final form, Daniel was written after the setting up of the altar to Olympian Zeus in the temple in December 167 BC (it is referred to as 'the abomination that makes desolate' in the book, 11: 31 and 12: 11) and before the re-dedication of the temple exactly three years later. The court tales in the first part of the book (to be discussed in greater detail in Chapter 6) probably circulated earlier than the visions, though they are quite closely linked with them. It is not difficult to see how they could have served to strengthen the faith of those who were suffering persecution. Daniel and his companions observed the food laws (1: 8–16), prayed three times a day (6: 10) and rejected idolatry even at risk of their lives (chapters 3 and 6). Like the visions which follow, the tales move in an atmosphere of divine mysteries, esoteric lore, dream interpretation, communion with angels and intense piety. The communications which the seer receives in visions promise an end to present tribulations. In the coded language of apocalyptic, they trace the course of events up to and beyond the time of writing, concluding with precise calculations of the imminent end of history and the coming of God's kingdom.

The author of Daniel clearly identified himself with those who were suffering persecution (11: 33-4) and dissociated himself from 'the men of violence among your own people' (11: 14), presumably the Hellenizers who supported Antiochus. The faithful addressed by him are 'the saints of the Most High' (7: 18, 21-2, 25) and 'the wise' (11: 33, 35; 12: 3, 10), though it is possible that the latter refers more specifically to the leaders of the group. That the apocalyptic seer's audience is the Asidaean assembly of 1 Maccabees is widely accepted and entirely plausible. The 'little help' which the persecuted are said to receive, and the adhesion to their cause of dubious allies (11: 34), would then refer to the Maccabees and their associates who joined the struggle *after* the persecution was under way. Since the statement that the tyrant will be broken by no human hand (8: 25) does not necessarily imply a pacifist or quietist posture, there is no incompatibility with the warlike character of the Asidaeans who, in any case, fought only by necessity and for much more limited objectives than the Maccabees.

Daniel, then, was written in and for an apocalyptic sect dedicated to upholding the holy covenant and the laws, practising its own kind of biblical interpretation (e.g. the author's re-interpretation of the seventy years of Jeremiah, Dan. 9: 1-2), and following its own sectarian *halakah* (legal interpretation). As such, it stands somewhere between the diaspora-group which supported the reforms of Ezra and the Qumran community established around the middle of the second century BC.

On the origins of the sects mentioned by Josephus (Essenes, Pharisees, Sadducees) there is much uncertainty. While the precise sequence of events is unknown, the Essenes probably originated as a branch of the Asidaeans who broke with the Maccabee leadership after Jonathan assumed the high priestly office around the middle of the second century BC. As described by the Jewish authors Josephus and Philo and the Roman naturalist Pliny the Elder, they formed communities of ascetics both in the cities and in the Judaean wilderness by the Dead Sea. Their lives were governed by a strict interpretation of the laws, especially the laws of purity, in addition to which they cherished their own esoteric teachings which they were bound by the most solemn oaths not to disclose. Almost all contemporary scholars identify the community of the Qumran scrolls as a branch of the Essenes. The writings recovered from the caves since 1947, and especially the Community Rule, confirm that the principal activity of the group was the study of Torah, which served as a substitute for participation in temple worship. Their founder, the Teacher of Righteousness, was above all a faithful interpreter of the law, and the task of authoritative legal exposition was continued by the Zadokite priests who formed the leadership. As in the days of Ezra and Nehemiah, the members entered into a covenant confirmed by oath:

> Whoever approaches the Council of the Community shall enter the Covenant of God in the presence of all who have freely pledged themselves. He shall undertake by a binding oath to return with all his heart and soul to every commandment of the Law of Moses in accordance with all that has been revealed of it to the sons of Zadok, the Keepers of the Covenant and Seekers of His will, and to the multitude of the men of their Covenant who together have freely pledged themselves to His truth and to walking in the way of His delight. And he shall undertake by the Covenant to separate from all the men of falsehood who walk in the way of wickedness. (Community Rule 5: 7–11)

It is important to note that the members committed themselves not just to Torah in general but to a particular interpretation of the laws. Something of this sectarian *halakah* can be found in the different community rules which have survived, and especially in the Damascus Rule, so called on account of the allusion in it to a new covenant made in the land of Damascus, possibly a symbolic name for Qumran. The sect's interpretation is, in general, stricter than that of the Pharisees, especially with regard to sabbath and ritual cleanness. While, for example, the Pharisees would allow an animal to be pulled out of a pit on the sabbath (see Mt. 12: 11), the Damascus Rule forbade it (11: 13–14). The most recently published and the longest of the Qumran texts, the so-called Temple Scroll containing sixty-seven columns, goes to extreme lengths to preserve not only the temple precincts but also the entire city from any taint of ritual impurity. To cite only one example: a man who has had sexual relations with his wife must wait three days to enter the holy city (column 45: 11-12). It is clear that, for the sectarians, these stipulations were on the same level as Pentateuchal law. One of the most surprising aspects of the Temple Scroll is that it contains, in effect, an *emended* version of parts of the Deuteronomic law attributed not, as in Deuteronomy, to Moses but to God himself.

This text, which is only beginning to be studied, provides yet another example of the remarkable variety of viewpoints with respect to the law in the late Second Temple period. We find a somewhat different perspective among the Pharisees whose early history is, unfortunately, not well known. As far as we can tell, they constituted a predominantly lay movement which emerged from the matrix of Hasidism during the early Hasmonaean period, though probably later than the Essenes. Reacting to the widespread secularization of the priesthood, the Pharisees (the word probably means 'separatists') sought to apply the purity laws encumbent on the priesthood to the entire people, and thus to realize the ideal of 'a kingdom of priests, a holy nation' (Ex. 19: 6). They were organized in associations based on table fellowship – the table representing the altar – and were committed to laws governing diet, tithing, purity, and conduct in general. The Pharisees were not on principle opposed to the priesthood – indeed, several priests joined their ranks – but the movement marked a decisive shift towards a lay religion which has characterized Judaism – and differentiated it from Christianity – ever since.

In pursuit of their ideals the Pharisees engaged in an intense campaign of religious education, recruiting disciples and teaching in the synagogues around the land. Some important aspects of the way in which they understood themselves and their mission are captured in the opening sentence of the Mishnaic treatise 'The Sayings of the Fathers' (*Pirke Aboth*):

> Moses received Torah from Sinai and delivered it to Joshua; then Joshua to the elders, the elders to the prophets, and the prophets delivered it to the men of the Great Assembly. They

said three things: be deliberate in judgment, raise up many disciples, and make a hedge for the Torah.

These three injunctions correspond to important functions of the scribe in the last days of the Second Temple: counsel in the administration of justice, teaching, and legal exposition. The 'hedge' is the complex of legal exegesis which safeguards the integrity of the biblical laws and, at the same time, applies them realistically to the actual situations of everyday life.

We must not be misled by the anti-Pharisaic polemic in the gospels into misrepresenting the intent and the effect of this teaching. As is now generally recognized, much of this polemic reflects the growing alienation between the Christian movement and the Jewish leadership which led to the Jewish–Christian schism in the decades following the great war with Rome. As against the Sadducees, who insisted on the letter of the law supplemented by their own decrees, the Pharisees developed a wide-ranging and complex *halakah* the purpose of which was to apply the laws humanely to concrete situations. The goal, we might say, was to make the law really work, and thus to bring the whole of life into conformity with the will of God. The measure of success achieved by this programme will be appreciated when we recall that it survived the disastrous wars with Rome to give shape and character to Jewish life in the reconstruction which followed.

6

Theological Wisdom

The confluence of wisdom and law

At the end of the first chapter we invited the reader to think of
wisdom and law as two great rivers which eventually flow together
and find their outlet in rabbinic writings and early Christian theology.
At different points in their development also, the sapiential and
legal traditions as represented in Old Testament writings make
contact with each other or follow parallel courses. We have noted,
for example, some interesting formal similarities between case law
and popular proverbial sayings, and between apodictic sentences of
law and the instruction. These have led to the suggestion that, in
its earliest stages, Israelite law can be seen as a specialization of
clan wisdom. We have also noted that the different collections of
laws invariably contain more than just legal enactments. Our brief
study of these collections, all the way from the Covenant Code
to the Damascus Rule and Temple Scroll from Qumran, has shown
that they cannot be described purely and simply as law codes.
In their care to provide appropriate motivation for observing the
laws and to promote a reflective approach to law-observance in
general, we have seen that they come close in several respects to the
teaching of the sages.

The same observation holds for the tendency to generalize, to
state the essence of the laws in a few basic principles, a tendency
which we have also noted throughout our study. When the great
Hillel reduced the 613 laws of the Pentateuch to the Golden Rule,
or when Jesus expressed the essence of the law in the command to
love God and the neighbour (Mt. 22: 34–40), they were simply
following a precedent set by the prophets and the sages. This would
suggest that the teaching of the sages entered the mainstream of

Israelite religion at the point where it came together with the legal tradition.

It was also noted that the publication of Deuteronomy marked an important point in the process which brought these two traditions together. While the book cannot simply be described as a product of scribalism, its emphasis on teaching and instruction brings to mind the practice of the sages. When Israel observes the laws it is recognized as a wise nation (Deut. 4: 6-7) and when it neglects them it is guilty of folly (32: 28-9). With regard to the understanding of wisdom, the book also contains a hint of later developments where it describes the law as revealed and accessible:

> For this commandment which I command you this day is not too hard for you, neither is it far off. It is not in heaven, that you should say, 'Who will go up for us to heaven, and bring it to us, that we may hear it and do it?' Neither is it beyond the sea, that you should say, 'Who will go over the sea for us, and bring it to us, that we may hear it and do it?' But the word is very near you; it is in your mouth and in your heart, so that you can do it. (Deut. 30: 11-14)

So there is a hidden wisdom, an esoteric knowledge, which God has not chosen to reveal, over against knowledge of the law which is all that Israel needs. The distinction is explicit at a different point in Moses's final address:

> The secret things belong to Yahweh our God; but the things that are revealed belong to us and to our children for ever, that we may do all the words of this law. (29: 29)

There is contained here, by implication, a new perception of the nature of wisdom which would generate new insights and problems. The true wisdom is a divine prerogative which is available to humankind only as God chooses to reveal it. As the author sees it, that part of divine wisdom which he has chosen to reveal is contained in the law. The law is therefore *the* expression of divine wisdom made available to Israel and, as such, can compete on more than equal terms with the vaunted wisdom of the nations. Nothing is said about the 'secret things' or, in other words, that part of wisdom which remains hidden with God, and nothing is said about any disposition made by God for the guidance of those outside Israel. We must now go on to see how these issues were developed by certain scribes and sages of the Second Temple period. Since an exhaustive analysis is not possible, we shall have to concentrate on a few texts which reflect more directly on the nature of wisdom and attempt to follow up whatever leads they may offer us.

Job 28: inaccessible wisdom

In the context of the dialogue or debate, the poem on wisdom in Job 28 is ascribed to Job himself (27: 1). But, immediately preceding chapter 28 is a passage (27: 13-23) in which the evildoer gets his just desserts. This could hardly have been spoken by Job who has expended a great deal of energy in denying precisely that. More probably, then, it belongs to the contribution of Zophar which, as we saw earlier (see p. 53), has been somewhat scrambled in transmission. We also saw that chapter 28 is generally thought to have existed independently and to have been provided with a conclusion more consonant with orthodox piety (28: 28). For that conclusion, which equates the fear of Yahweh with wisdom, not only seems inappropriate coming from Job at that point in the book but does not make an easy fit with the rest of the poem.

Using the powerful metaphor of mining, the poet begins by describing what is involved in obtaining silver, gold, and precious ore: working long hours underground, far from the haunts of everyday life, in constant danger and, above all, in isolation:

> That path no bird of prey knows,
>   and the falcon's eye has not seen it.
> The proud beasts have not trodden it;
>   The lion has not passed over it.   (vv. 7-8)

The genesis of this image may, perhaps, be found in those proverbs and instructions which compare wisdom with precious metals:

> Happy is the man who finds wisdom,
>   and the man who gets understanding,

> For the gain from it is better than gain from silver,
>   and its profit better than gold.
> She is more precious than jewels,
>   and nothing you desire can compare with her.
>   (Prov. 3: 13–15)

The point is that if such a price must be paid to obtain precious metals from the earth, how much more difficult must it be to acquire wisdom? There is no comforting answer to the question which is then posed as a refrain in the poem:

> Where shall wisdom be found?
>   and where is the place of understanding?
>   (vv. 12, 20)

It is not in the land of the living, nor in the heights and depths of the cosmos, nor in those dark waters with which the Hebrew imagination surrounded the inhabited world. There exists no currency with which it may be purchased or against which it may even be appraised. Even Death, who presides over all, has heard but a rumour of it (v. 22).

The conclusion of the poem is that only God knows and possesses wisdom since only he was present at the creation when he saw it and appraised it (vv. 23–7). This image of wisdom present with God in the act of creation is consonant with the mythological scenario described in the divine answer to Job quoted in the previous chapter (Job 38: 4–7). The cosmos is a great temple and its construction is rounded off with a ceremony of dedication at which the 'sons of God', members of the divine retinue, engage with joyful song in the liturgy. The earthly counterpart is, of course, the dedication of Solomon's temple (1 Kgs. 8) and of the rebuilt temple after the return from exile (Ezra 3: 10–13). There is therefore in the poem at least a hint of wisdom personified participating in some way in the work of creation, a hint which will be more fully developed in another composition to be considered shortly (Prov. 8: 22–31).

After this strong statement about the absence of wisdom, the finale can hardly fail to sound somewhat anti-climactic and even incongruous:

> And he said to man,
> 'Behold, the fear of Yahweh, that is wisdom;
>   and to depart from evil is understanding.'
>   (v. 28)

Almost all commentators agree that these lines have been added as a sort of nervous corrective to the negative verdict on the human quest for wisdom in the body of the poem. After all, it was axiomatic with the sages that the search for wisdom would not go unrewarded:

> If you seek it like silver
>   and search for it as for hidden treasures;
> Then you will understand the fear of Yahweh,
>   and find the knowledge of God.   (Prov. 2: 4)

It is also worthy of note that the same language of fearing Yahweh and turning from evil occurs in the narrative prologue where Yahweh turns to the Satan and says:

> Have you considered my servant Job, that there is none like him on the earth, a blameless and upright man, *who fears God and turns away from evil*?   (1: 8)

This might suggest that the same author who provided the dialogue with its narrative framework also felt it necessary to end the poem in this way, consonant with the final form of the book. That this was the conventional solution may be seen in an admonition in Proverbs which might have been written expressly for Job (italics mine):

> Trust in Yahweh with all your heart,
>   and do not rely on your own insight.
> In all your ways acknowledge him,
>   and he will make straight your paths.
> Be not wise in your own eyes;
>   *fear Yahweh and turn away from evil.*
> It will be healing for your flesh,
>   and refreshment to your bones.   (3: 5–8)

This answer of conventional piety which, faithful to the perspectives of Deuteronomy, equates wisdom with doing good and avoiding evil and therefore, in effect, with observing the law, makes a point which is by no means trivial. Given the problematic nature of experience it is not, however, a completely adequate answer. That, as we saw earlier (pp. 52ff.), is the whole point of the dialogue in Job. If, then, we turn to consider the poem in its original form, without the 'orthodox' ending, we can see how it could have functioned as a criticism of Job who, misled by the rationalist creed of the sages to whose ranks he belonged, assumed that the problems posed by experience should always yield to intellectual enquiry. If, however, one ascribes the poem to Zophar, it would serve as an indictment of Job's refusal to accept the mysterious ways of God. It would be a reminder both to him and to his colleagues that the kind of wisdom necessary for solving the problem posed by his experience, for reducing it to some semblance of rationality, was simply not available.

If this interpretation is correct, it is really not very important to decide whether the poem was interpolated or not. Much of the imagery is, in any case, found elsewhere in the book, and Job's partners in dialogue refer more than once to the divine wisdom manifested in creation (e.g. 26: 5-14; 36: 24-33; 37: 1-24). Zophar himself had already made the same point, with the same implications, in a somewhat different way:

> Oh, that God would speak,
>   and open his lips to you,
> and that he would tell you the secrets of wisdom!
>   For he is manifold in understanding . . .
> Can you find out the deep things of God?
>   Can you find out the limits of the Almighty?
> It is higher than heaven — what can you do?
>   Deeper than Sheol — what can you know?   (11: 5-8)

Zophar's prayer was answered and God did speak; but he said nothing which had not been said already in the book (38: 1 – 40: 2). If Job was satisfied, it was not because of what was said, but because of who said it:

> I had heard of thee by the hearing of the ear,
>   but now my eye sees thee . . .   (42: 5)

The world-wide search for wisdom of which the poem speaks is consonant with the practice, common to the sages, of interrogating nature for clues to rational order and analogies to the moral life. It is clear, though, that this whole procedure has now become quite problematic. Nature does not so easily render up its secrets to human reason confident of its own powers. On the contrary, it itself poses questions which call for a deeper level of reflection.

Proverbs 8: 22–31: Wisdom, firstborn of creation

Something has already been said of the first part of Proverbs (1–9) in an earlier chapter (see pp. 136ff.). To sum it up briefly, it is thought by many to be the work of the same author who assembled the various components of Proverbs and would therefore be quite late, perhaps as late as the Hellenistic period. It would have been placed at the beginning as a kind of theological preface to the other instructions and anthologies of proverbs. If this is so, and we cannot be sure, the section is certainly not all of a piece with respect to genre, style, and content.

Before looking at the two quite distinctive passages in which Wisdom speaks and is spoken of as a person (1: 20–33 and 8: 1–36), we should note the theme which runs through the instructions in the rest of the section: that of the foreign woman, Wisdom's shadow (2: 16–19; 5: 3–23; 6: 24–35; 7: 5–27; 9: 13–18). Her seductive arts are described graphically and in some detail. There is even the motif, common to ancient and modern fiction, of the husband absent on business (7: 19–20). We would therefore be led to think of this portrait as serving the purpose of moral admonition, and, indeed, the point about marital infidelity is made explicitly and in moralizing terms (5: 15–20; 6: 25–35). If, however, we recall the frequent association in the Hebrew Bible between sexual immorality and idolatry (e.g. 1 Kgs. 11: 1–9 and Hos. 1–3), we shall probably agree that this portrait of the *femme fatale* also stands for the allure of foreign cults and therefore warns against *religious* infidelity. One has only to think of the foreign wives of Esau and Solomon or the measures taken by Ezra with respect to such unions.

Even if the passages which speak of Wisdom as a person are not editorial additions, as many commentators argue, the figure of Wisdom may well have been suggested by the counter-image of the foreign woman. Both have their house, both offer love (e.g. 4: 6-9) and can be addressed as lover or bride (e.g. 7: 4), though while union with the one leads to death, the other offers life. Wisdom (*hokmah*, a feminine noun in Hebrew) is presented with all the positive aspects of femininity. Like the good woman described at the end of the book, she is 'more precious than pearls' (31: 10; cf. 3: 15; 8: 11; Job 28: 18), a phrase which seems to have been proverbial in Israel for a good wife.

The passages in which Wisdom speaks with her own voice are quite different from those in which the sage speaks about her. In the first of these (1: 20-33) she addresses the uninstructed in the market place or the city gate, or anywhere where people tend to gather. While she speaks in her own person, and speaks of Yahweh in the third person, it is tolerably clear that her discourse is modelled on prophetic speech. When, for example, she says that

> They will call upon me, but I will not answer;
> They will seek me diligently but will not find me
> (1: 28)

we are reminded of such prophetic announcements as:

> Then you shall call, and Yahweh will answer;
> you shall cry, and he will say, Here I am.
> (Is. 58: 9)

or

> I was ready to be sought by those who did not ask
> for me;
> I was ready to be found by those who did not
> seek me.
> I said, 'Here am I, here am I'
> to a nation that did not call my name.   (Is. 65: 1)

The same kind of speech is continued in 8: 1-21, though it is clearer that what is being offered in this passage is wisdom, of the kind which enables kings to rule well and which leads to material prosperity. The mixture of the prophetic and sapiential in these discourses provides one of several indications that, by the time of writing, the sages had begun to assume for their own teaching the kind of absolute authority claimed by the great prophets of the past. A similar claim is advanced here and there by the sages who debated with Job (e.g. 4: 12-21), and Ben Sira will compare his scribal teaching explicitly with prophecy (Ecclus. 24: 33). For an even later period there is the rabbinic dictum (in the Talmudic treatise Baba Bathra 12a) that prophecy has been taken from the prophets and given to the sages.

The second discourse of Wisdom takes a quite different and un-unexpected direction (8: 22-31); so much so, that several commentators have felt obliged to conclude that it must have been interpolated. Wisdom declares that she came into existence at the beginning of creation and that she was present with God during the work of creation. There is a certain studied ambiguity in speaking of *how* Wisdom came into existence, owing to the fact that – as we shall see – the poet is taking over and adapting a theogony, a type of myth which speaks of the birth of gods and goddesses. It is also less than clear what role, if any, Wisdom played in the work of creation. The Greek translator – followed by RSV – interprets the end of the passage in the sense that Wisdom acted as God's agent and artificer:

> Then I was beside him, like a master workman;
> and I was daily his delight,
>   rejoicing before him always,
> rejoicing in his inhabited world
>   and delighting in the sons of men. (vv. 30-1)

In other words, she was commissioned to do the work in much the same way that Moses commissioned Bezalel – an artificer full of the Spirit and of wisdom (Ex. 35: 31) – to make the wilderness sanctuary and its furniture. This, however, is to ignore the context which conveys rather the image of a favourite child who delights her father and takes pleasure in what he has made. Here, too, the obscurity may be due to the inappropriate representation of Yahweh as a god who begets offspring.

The literary form, according to which something or someone

is created *before* a series of other things (vv. 22-6), is a first clue to the mythic character of this representation. It can be verified, for example, in the opening of the canonical Babylonian creation myth (called *enuma elish* from its opening words) and is reflected in the introduction to the Eden myth in Genesis (2: 4-5). Since Wisdom is a person begotten at the beginning of time, the specific form of the myth is a theogony, amply attested in ancient Mesopotamia, Egypt, and Greece. The closest parallel known to us from cultures familiar to Israel and early Judaism is the Egyptian myth of the birth of the goddess Maat from the sun god Re. His favourite child, she came down to mankind at the beginning of time as the embodiment of cosmic order and the preserver of law and justice. During the Hellenistic period Maat was identified with the great Egyptian goddess Isis whose cult was extremely popular throughout the Mediterranean world, nowhere more so than in the Ptolemaic Empire to which Judah belonged during the third century BC. Since this provides a quite plausible date for the poem, there seems no good reason to deny the possibility of such a borrowing.

What, then, we would have in Prov. 8: 22-31 is what Plato called philosophizing by means of myth or, in other words, a reflective use of mythological themes and constructs to draw conclusions which retain their vitality outside the world of myth. This should not be surprising, since it is found throughout the Old Testament beginning with the primeval history in Gen. 1-11. It would, on the contrary, be surprising if Israel's sages denied themselves this mode of reflection. The author of Prov. 1-9 introduces mythological motifs at many points. He speaks of the tree of life (11: 30), the fountain of life (13: 14), Wisdom's house with its seven pillars (7: 6, 8; 9: 1). The poem in chapter 8 is no more than an extension of this usage.

Despite the uncertainty about Wisdom as artificer, the sense is clearly that she presides over creation with God. To that extent we have moved beyond the perspective of Job 28 in which the search for her traces in nature proves to be unsuccessful. The point is made more clearly in a related fragment (Prov. 3: 19-20):

> Yahweh by wisdom founded the earth;
>> by understanding he established the heavens;
> by his knowledge the deeps broke forth,
>> and the clouds drop down the dew.

Wisdom, then, existed before everything else. Though created, her relationship with God is unique. She was with him at creation and in some way presided over it or co-operated with God in it. At the same time, her relation to the created order remains to be spelled out. We shall go on to see that, in spelling it out, both Jews and Christians elaborated some of their most central theological affirmations.

Ecclus. 24: 1-29: Torah assimilated to Wisdom

Ecclesiasticus is more of a book in the modern sense of the word than any of the compositions we have seen so far. We know the author's name from the epilogue to the original work (50: 27-9) and from the prologue to the Greek translation made by his grandson in Egypt some time after 132 BC. The author, a scribe and teacher called Jesus but more commonly known by his patronym Ben Sira, also introduces occasional autobiographical allusions from which we gather that he was getting on in years (8: 6), that he had knocked about in the world quite a bit (34: 9-12) and that, at the time of writing, he conducted a school or academy, presumably in Jerusalem (51: 23). The date of composition can also be established with a fair degree of accuracy. His historical survey ends with Simon II who was high priest at the time of the Seleucid conquest of Palestine (200-198 BC), and there is no allusion to the usurpation of the high priesthood by Jason at the beginning of the reign of Antiochus IV about a quarter of a century later. He wrote therefore about 180 BC, not long before the acute phase of the crisis brought on by the Hellenistic party in Jerusalem and the policies of Antiochus IV.

The author's conservative viewpoint may be deduced from the fact that he wrote in Hebrew at a time when it was quite common for Jewish authors to seek a broader audience for their works by writing in Greek, the language of the dominant culture. The same conclusion is suggested by his tireless insistence on 'the fear of Yahweh' as the basic principle of conduct and his denunciation of the impious who had abandoned the law (41: 8-10). He also takes issue with contemporary Jewish teachers who, misled by current philosophical trends, were denying free will and divine providence (e.g. 15: 11-20; 16: 17-23). His students are put on their guard against the dangers of philosophical speculation divorced from piety (3: 21-4); and it is possible that here and elsewhere he has Qoheleth in mind. His support of the Oniads, the legitimate high priestly family, went hand in hand with a moderate nationalism expressed in his prayer for deliverance from foreign rule (36: 1-17). We can only speculate on where he would have stood during the crisis which broke over Jews in the homeland not much more than a decade after he wrote his book.

Ben Sira was evidently concerned to respond to the challenge posed by Greek culture, but to do it in his own way. This is already suggested by the prologue which identifies Israel's wisdom as the law, the prophets, and the other writings. For the author himself the law is only part, although the most important part, of the curriculum which he teaches (39: 1-5). As much as he insists on the observance of the commandments, it is clear that the category which dominates his thinking is not the law but wisdom. The structure of the book points unequivocally in this direction. It begins with a paean of praise for wisdom (1: 1-10), concludes with an acrostic poem describing his own lifelong search for it (51: 13-30), and has for its centrepiece the great apostrophe of wisdom (24: 1-29), discussed more in detail below (pp. 142-4). This enables us to read the book as a defence of Judaism, based on the argument that Israel has its own wisdom which is superior to that of the Greeks. Josephus will take the same line in his treatise *Against Apion* following what was, in effect, a major point of Jewish polemic in late antiquity.

The opening statement (1: 1-10) makes it clear at once that, unlike the sages of an earlier day, Ben Sira regards wisdom as belonging to the divine world and available to humankind only as a gift. There is therefore a close parallelism between wisdom and the Spirit and, correspondingly, between the one endowed with wisdom and the prophet. Hence the author can speak of himself being filled with the spirit of understanding (39: 6) and pouring out his teaching like prophecy (24: 33). Following Prov. 8: 22–31, he represents wisdom as first of all created things and the principle which informs the created order:

> Yahweh himself created wisdom;
>   he saw her and apportioned her,
>   he poured her out upon all his works. (1: 9)

Following upon this, he is at pains throughout his work to defend the goodness and order of a world created by means of divine wisdom — a point by no means obvious to many of his contemporaries. While his starting point is in the creation narratives in Genesis 1–2 which he paraphrases in his own way (unlike the modern biblical scholar, he reads them as one and undivided), his concern is to account for evil without imputing it to the Creator. An interesting argument along this line is that, while all things must come from God, nothing can exist without its antithesis; evil, therefore, is a necessary part of the created order:

> Good is the opposite of evil,
>   and life the opposite of death;
>   so the sinner is the opposite of the godly.
> Look upon all the works of the Most High;
>   they likewise are in pairs, one the opposite
>   of the other. (33: 14–15)
>
> All things are twofold, one opposite the other,
>   and he has made nothing incomplete. (42: 24)

Whatever we may think of this argument, it shows the author attempting to re-state traditional texts in a more universally comprehensible language. A quite different but equally interesting example would be his survey of the national history (44–49). Departing quite radically from the mainline historiographical tradition represented by the Chronicler, he presents it in the form of short biographies, in keeping with a literary genre which was at that time beginning to come into its own.

The central statement of the book — literally, since it comes in the middle (chapter 24) — is the apostrophe of personified Wisdom delivered in the divine assembly. In exalted language she tells how she proceeded from the mouth of God in the very beginning of time, before anything was created; how she came down from her throne on the pillar of cloud to wander through the world in search of a resting place; and how her search ended when she was established in the sanctuary of 'the beloved city', Jerusalem:

> Then the Creator of all things gave me a commandment,
> > and the one who created me assigned a place for my
> > > tent.
> And he said, 'Make your dwelling in Jacob,
> > and in Israel receive your inheritance.' . . .
> In the holy tabernacle I ministered before him,
> > and so I was established in Zion.
> In the beloved city likewise he gave me a resting place,
> > and in Jerusalem was my dominion.
> So I took root in an honoured people,
> > in the portion of Yahweh who is their inheritance.
>
> (24: 8–12)

It will be noted that, unlike Prov. 8: 22–31, the author draws freely on the historical and cultic traditions of Israel. Comparison is, nevertheless, inevitable. Here too, in all probability, Wisdom is modelled on the goddess Isis, or perhaps a Syro-Palestinian counterpart like Astarte, whose cults were very popular at the time. Texts have come down to us in which the goddess Isis declares her own praises in the first person, describes how she presided over creation as the eldest daughter of Re (identified with Chronos), and how she descended from her heavenly abode to search through the world for a place in which to establish her cult. Both formally and thematically the self-praise of Wisdom in Ecclus. 24 is so close to these aretalogies, as they are called, that several scholars have concluded that it was probably modelled on them. There can be little doubt, at any rate, that he has taken over the figure of Wisdom in Prov. 8 and developed it in his own way.

The novel element in Ben Sira's thinking is seen in the second part of the poem in which he identifies this pre-existent, immortal Wisdom with Torah:

> All this is the book of the covenant of the Most
>   High God,
> the law which Moses commanded us
> as an inheritance for the congregation of Jacob.
>
>   (v. 23)

The identification follows naturally enough from the figure used in the first half of the poem, since Isis (Maat) stood for cosmic order and presided over justice and the administration of law. It was therefore Ben Sira's way of attributing universal significance to Torah as the divine principle of order which has been made available to Israel. Indirectly, therefore, it refuted the charge of particularism levelled at the law by both Gentiles and 'enlightened' contemporary Jewish intellectuals.

The manner in which Israel received the law as an unsolicited gift is expressed in a kind of poetic midrash on the four rivers of Eden in Gen. 2: 10–14:

> It fills men with wisdom, like the Pishon,
>   and like the Tigris at the time of the first fruits.
> It makes them full of understanding, like the Euphrates,
>   and like the Jordan at harvest time.
> It makes instruction shine forth like light,
>   like the Gihon at the time of vintage.
> Just as the first man did not know her perfectly,
>   the last one has not fathomed her;
> for her thought is more abundant than the sea,
>   and her counsel deeper than the great abyss.
>
>   (24: 25–9)

Continuing the metaphor, he speaks of himself, as sage and teacher, drawing water from this inexhaustible source to irrigate his own plot, that is, his school, becoming in the process a source of life and growth in his own right. No better metaphor could be thought of for the tradition of Torah-learning inherited and advanced by Ben Sira: a mighty river with tributaries and canals, bringing life to the land through which it passes.

While this kind of speculation about wisdom and law was going on in academic and intellectual circles, it was not without effect on worship and piety. The psalms often speak of the law and several of them — including Ps. 119, the longest — reflect on Torah as a divine gift. The tone is set in Ps. 1, probably intended as an introduction to the book, in which the metaphor used by Ben Sira is applied to the faithful who meditate day and night on the law:

> he is like a tree
> planted by streams of water,
> that yields its fruit in its season,
> and its leaf does not wither.

The division into five books, though of uncertain date, also underlines the connection between law and worship since it is clearly modelled on the Pentateuchal 'five fifths of the law'. Even a rapid glance at the Jewish Daily Prayer Book (the *Siddur*) will suffice to show that, in the actual practice of religion, piety and Torah-study are still integrally related.

The Wisdom of Solomon — towards a new synthesis

The different strands of reflection and speculation woven by the sages whose compositions we have been discussing cannot easily be brought together into a cohesive philosophy or theology based on wisdom. By the time of Ben Sira, Jewish philosophers, especially in Alexandria, were beginning to reformulate Torah-religion as a philosophy. We know some of their names but their works have survived, if at all, only in fragments. Ben Sira himself was no philosopher, even though he attempted in his own way to respond to the Greek 'enlightenment'. His identification of wisdom with law, nonetheless, influenced several Jewish writers whose work has survived from the two and a half centuries preceding the destruction of the Second Temple.

One of these writers was the author of a short work which is listed in the Apocrypha under the name of Baruch. It purports to come from the hand of Jeremiah's companion and scribe, but was in fact written by an anonymous Jew some time during the Hasmonaean principate. It contains a poem, of no great originality, which describes wisdom as unknown to the nations of the world, even those famous for wisdom like the Edomites, and undiscovered throughout the course of history prior to the appearance of Israel on the scene (3: 9 – 4: 4). This wisdom, which was with God from the beginning, then came down to earth and lived among humankind in the guise of the Torah:

> She is the book of the commandments of God,
>   and the law that endures for ever.
> All who hold fast to her will live,
>   and those who forsake her will die.   (4: 1)

While the influence of Ben Sira will be noted at once, the pattern of pre-existence, descent into the world and embodiment in Torah is more clearly expressed. This pattern, based on a mythic model as we have seen, will in due course provide early Christian writers with a language in which to speak of the identity and mission of Jesus.

The nature and role of wisdom are elaborated much more ambitiously and at much greater length in another work, written about a century later, for Greek-speaking Jews and interested non-Jews living in Egypt. Following the example of Proverbs, Ecclesiastes, and the Song of Songs, the author places his work within the sapiential tradition by donning the mantle of Solomon; hence the title The Wisdom of Solomon which the work now bears. The first part of the book consists of two lengthy discourses of Solomon to his fellow-rulers (1-5 and 6-9). The first of these contrasts the fate of the impious, who justify their conduct on the basis of the Epicurean doctrine of fate, with that of the faithful whom they persecute and put to death. The decisive factor in the author's argument, and a new one as far as we know, is the immortality of the soul, by virtue of which the death of the just is seen as the entrance to a blessed eternity.

The second of the two discourses, in which the writer for the first time identifies himself with Solomon, narrates how he acquired wisdom in answer to prayer. After listing the twenty-one attributes of wisdom (based on a well-known Stoic hymn to Zeus), he goes on to state how it proceeds from God as a spiritual essence and passes into the souls of those disposed to receive it. The last part of the work (10-19) deals with the role of wisdom in history from creation to the exodus. It includes a lengthy diatribe against the stupidity of idolatry, singling out as the most stupid kind the Egyptian worship of animals (theriolatry).

While modern commentators have not generally been impressed by the philosophical depth and acumen of this work, it can be argued that its attempt to place the Jewish religion within a broad philosophical context is, in some respects, remarkably innovative. It will be noticed that, in spite of the author's spirited defence of Jewish martyrs (whether in Judah or Egypt cannot be determined) and detestation of idolatry, he hardly ever alludes to the law except in passing (2: 12; 6: 4; 16: 6). He does not even mention it in speaking of Moses's leadership of Israel in the wilderness (10: 15 — 11: 14), and Moses himself is described not as a lawgiver but a prophet (11: 1). He does speak of *wisdom's* laws, in a passage in which traditional and non-traditional themes are brought together elegantly in the rhetorical figure of speech known as sorites:

> The beginning of wisdom is the most sincere desire for
>   instruction,
> and concern for instruction is love of her,
> and love of her is the keeping of her laws,
> and giving heed to her laws is assurance of immortality,
> and immortality brings one near to God;
> so the desire for wisdom leads to a kingdom.   (6: 17–20)

This form of argument, dear to Stoic preachers and familiar to Paul (e.g. Rom. 5: 3–5), provides an interesting example of theological re-statement. The laws in question, wisdom's laws, certainly include the stipulations of Torah, as the allusion to Deut. 11: 1 makes clear: 'You shall therefore love Yahweh your God, and keep his . . . commandments always.' They are, however, put into a broader context by being derived from wisdom as cosmic principle. Correspondingly, the author's ethic is not limited to Torah and the *halakah*. Much of it, in fact, has close affinity with Stoic moral philosophy, e.g., the cardinal virtues of self-control, prudence, justice and courage (8: 7).

A further implication is that Torah-observance, far from being a petty, provincial affair, is Israel's way of being true to the order and harmony of the world. Like the world-soul of the Stoics, the wisdom of which the author speaks 'reaches mightily from one end of the earth to the other, ordering all things well' (8: 1). Following Ecclus. 24, he portrays her as initiated into divine knowledge and as artificer of the created world (8: 4). She is therefore the source not only of the laws but also of the encyclopaedic knowledge which the tradition attributed to Solomon (7: 15-22). Her relationship to God is expressed in an accumulation of metaphors:

> For she is a breath of the power of God,
> and a pure emanation of the glory of the Almighty;
> therefore nothing defiled gains entrance into her.
> For she is a reflection of eternal light,
> a spotless mirror of the working of God,
> an image of his goodness.   (7: 25-6)

This kind of language is reminiscent of Greek philosophical teachings on the mind (*nous*) or active principle (*logos*) of the world. Its eventual contribution to Christian theology, especially the doctrine of the Holy Spirit and the nature of Christ, is apparent already in the New Testament.

In the older wisdom, ethical instruction provided the link between cosmic order and the life of the individual. Wisdom denoted a certain quality of life which could be attained by the application of reason and the expenditure of effort. The readings so far in this chapter will have shown how different the situation was for those teachers of a later time for whom wisdom belonged to the divine world and was attainable only as a gift of God. Following their lead, the author of the Wisdom of Solomon describes how the great king achieved union with her as a result of searching and praying (7: 7; 9: 1-18). He believes that there is an innate bond between the human soul and wisdom. Souls are created immortal, since they are in the image of the immortal God; only at a later point did death enter in through the devil in the guise of the tempting serpent (2: 23-4); cf. Gen. 1:26-7; 3:1 – an interesting example of the author's exegesis). Following Plato, he holds that the soul existed as a spiritual essence before entering into a perishable body (8: 19-20; 9: 15). The possession of wisdom is the pledge that the original destiny of the human person will be restored (6: 17-20; 8: 13, 17).

Wisdom also is a spiritual entity since it is identical with the divine Spirit:

> Who has learned thy counsel,
>   unless thou hast given wisdom
>   and sent thy holy Spirit from on high?   (9: 17)

This 'spirit of wisdom' (7: 7) enters the souls of the devout, bringing with it what Christians will call 'the gifts of the Spirit':

> In every generation she passes into holy souls
> and makes them friends of God, and prophets.
>   (7: 27)

The same perspective on wisdom as the divine Spirit and as the source of the holy life is also found in the works of the Jewish philosopher Philo of Alexandria (*c*. 20 BC to AD 50). While literary dependence of Philo on Wisdom has not been established, it is clear that Alexandria was one of the principal centres where this work of philosophical and theological synthesis was going on. It was there that Ben Sira's book was translated into Greek and that Wisdom, in all probability, was composed. After Philo, and greatly influenced by him, there arose there one of the most influential of early Christian theological schools represented by Clement and Origen.

In the second part of Wisdom (10-19) the author introduces wisdom under a different aspect, i.e., as the active principle in sacred history. Something of this can be detected already in Baruch, but the author of Wisdom takes in the entire span from creation to the exodus, using his concept of wisdom as a principle of interpretation or re-interpretation. His method is quite different from the allegorical exegesis of Philo and early Christian writers. It is comparable to, but not identical with, the haggadic midrash already being practised in Judaism. But the author's very specific intent of 'sapientializing' biblical history results in a kind of treatise which is really *sui generis*. It is also dictated by the polemical needs of the situation in which he wrote. Hence his emphasis on the Egyptian phase of Israel's history and his taking a quite disproportionate amount of space and time to refute and ridicule idolatry, especially the kind practised in Egypt at that time.

Daniel: apocalyptic wisdom

Using a selection of the texts which have survived, some in the Hebrew Bible and others outside it, we have traced one line of development in the intellectual and religious history of Judaism during the last centuries of the Second Temple. The presence in the third part of the canon (the Writings) of a quite different kind of composition, Daniel, indicates another direction taken by scribes and sages at that time, and one no less important for the future.

Daniel is an apocalypse, which means that it treats of divine mysteries concerned primarily with the course of the future as revealed to chosen intermediaries. The additions in the Septuagint (the Prayer of Azariah, the Song of the Three Youths, Susanna, Bel and the Dragon) and certain fragments discovered at Qumran (especially the Prayer of Nabonidus which has affinities with Dan. 4) suggest that the biblical book was part of a larger Daniel cycle. No other apocalyptic compositions from the Hellenistic period were admitted into the canon, though we may be sure that others were produced. The much larger cycle dealing with Enoch, the sage of the archaic period who was taken up into heaven (Gen. 5: 18-24), contains sections which are almost certainly older than Daniel which can be dated to about 165 BC. All of this material deals in one way or another with divinely imparted wisdom, but the point of view is significantly different from that of the texts which we have been discussing in this chapter.

Debate on the origins of apocalyptic has, in recent years, tended to focus on the question whether it developed from prophecy or wisdom. Such a way of posing the issue is, however, over-simplified, especially when it gives the impression that we are dealing with three distinct and identifiable entities called prophecy, wisdom, and apocalyptic. It also tends to leave out of account the fact that apocalyptic is not confined to Judaism, being attested elsewhere (Persia, Babylon, Egypt) during the Hellenistic period. While there are obvious points of contact between prophecy and apocalyptic, the differences are no less significant, and it is misleading to represent the one deriving from the other by a gradual process of evolution.

One important point of contact between prophecy and apocalyptic is the claim, assumed by the writers of apocalyptic, to interpret prophetic texts by divine inspiration and warranty. It is by virtue of this claim that the author of Daniel, who presents himself as a sage, is able to predict the course of future events. We noted earlier how scribes and sages of the later period assume for their writings an inspiration and authority comparable to the prophetic claim. It is along this line that we can see a significant shift from inspired prophetic utterance to an interpretative activity for which a comparable inspiration is claimed. This is one important aspect of apocalyptic which is essential for understanding Daniel.

At first reading, the book seems to fall neatly into two parts: a series of court tales featuring Daniel and three companions (1–6) and four visions dealing with the course of history and its imminent consummation (7–12). A complicating factor, however, is the bilingual nature of the work, with Aramaic from Dan. 2: 4 (where the Babylonian sages reply to the king) to the end of the first vision (7: 28), and the rest of the book in Hebrew. This has led some to suspect that the first vision, the Four Beasts and the Son of Man (chapter 7), is meant to go with the court tales; and in fact there is a rather close parallelism between that vision and Nebuchadnezzar's dream of the statue made of four different metals (chapter 2). It should also be noted that the stories in the first part of the book are not all of the same kind. The second, fourth, and fifth illustrate Daniel's wisdom as interpreter of divine mysteries, while the first, third, and sixth are designed to show how God protects those who faithfully observe the laws, especially in the matter of false worship. The tales may well have circulated independently of and earlier than the visions, as was observed earlier. If so, they are now quite closely integrated with them, and their relevance to the situation of persecution in which the visions were written would have been immediately obvious.

Our present purpose will be satisfied if, in reading the book, we can discover what it means to be wise in this context and, especially, what is the origin and nature of the wisdom with which the principal characters are endowed. In the court tales the Jewish youths are 'skilful in all wisdom, endowed with knowledge, understanding and learning' (1: 4). Since they were put through a three-year curriculum in Babylonian science and letters — which would have included such subjects as astronomy and the interpretation of dreams and omens — their knowledge was not confined to their own religious tradition. In both the tales and the visions it is self-evident that wisdom and the life of holiness go together. Everything takes place in an atmosphere of observance, prayer, fasting, penitential exercises, visions, and communion with the unseen world. As noted in the previous chapter, Daniel was written in and for one of the pietist groups which opposed Antiochus IV and his Jewish collaborators. It is therefore feasible to see in this portrayal of the main characters a profile of the sectarian ideal. It is also possible that Daniel himself, who is carefully distinguished from his colleagues, stands for the leadership of the group. His distinctive competence is, at any rate, emphasized right from the start:

> As for these four youths, God gave them learning and skill in all letters and wisdom; and Daniel had understanding in all visions and dreams. (1: 17)

As we read on, we note that during the first crisis, precipitated by the mad king's decision to exterminate the sages, all of them prayed but the mystery was revealed only to Daniel in a vision, allowing him to interpret the dream of the statue (2: 17–45) and of the great tree (4: 19–27). During the reign of Belshazzar (mistakenly identified by the author as the son of Nebuchadnezzar) he was able to interpret the writing on the wall by virtue of his 'excellent spirit, knowledge, and understanding to interpret dreams, explain riddles, and solve problems' (5: 12). In the second part of the book Daniel alone appears, and it is he who has the visions in which the course of history and its future consummation are revealed. If the leaders of the group are the ones referred to as 'the wise' or, perhaps more exactly, 'the teachers' (*maskilim* in Hebrew: 11: 33, 35; 12: 3, 10), it would be natural to see them reflected in the visionary sage who is the hero of the book.

We noted a moment ago that inspired interpretation is an essential feature of apocalyptic. Unlike the prophet, the apocalyptic seer does not ascribe divine authority to his message in his own person, but claims rather to have received a revelation from one of the sages of the past, generally the very distant past. We thus have apocalyptic books under the name of Noah, Enoch, and even Adam. From this point of view Daniel is somewhat different since the author is represented as living during the Babylonian and early Persian periods. A heroic and wise figure bearing the name Dan'el features in one of the Bronze Age epics from Ugarit and is mentioned elsewhere in the Old Testament (Ezek. 28: 3 cf. 14: 14). In the Book of Jubilees, a sectarian composition from the second century BC, a Danel is the father-in-law of Enoch and is described as 'the first among men who learned writing and knowledge and wisdom' (4: 20). It may be that this tradition was transferred from the archaic period to the time of the exile because of the way in which the author of Daniel wished to narrate the course of history and depict Antiochus IV under the guise of the Babylonian tyrant Nebuchadnezzar. This, at any rate, provided him with a point of departure for his interpretation of history leading up to and beyond the dark hour through which Judaism was then passing.

If it is accepted that Daniel and his companions stand for the members of the group from which the book comes, it should be possible to find clues to the way its members carried on the all important activity of interpretation. The 'text' to be interpreted can be a dream or a vision. It can also be an actual written text: mysterious words which appear on a wall (5: 5-9), a Book of Truth preserved in heaven (10: 21) or, in one case only, a biblical text (9: 2). The important point is that (with the obvious exception of the heavenly book) the real meaning was unknown to the original author, being revealed for the first time to the inspired interpreter. We find the same kind of procedure in early Christianity and in the Qumran sect. A commentary on the prophet Habakkuk, discovered in the first cave of Qumran, makes the same assumption as the author of Daniel:

God told Habakkuk to write down what would come upon the last generation; but he did not reveal to him the consummation of the age. And when he (Habakkuk) said, 'so that he may run who reads it' (2: 2), its interpretation refers to the Teacher of Righteousness to whom God made known all the secrets of the words of his servants the prophets. (7: 1-5)

Something of the same formulation is already apparent in Daniel: here is the dream; this is its interpretation. In Daniel, as at Qumran, the text is interpreted atomistically, in the sense that each item in the dream, vision or writing is given its own separate referent. Each part of the great statue, for example, corresponds to a specific kingdom and phase of history. The interpretation can also take place during or shortly after a visionary experience; and a further complication is that the vision itself is sometimes explained by a heavenly intermediary — generally Gabriel — who is himself an actor in the vision.

We have looked into the matter of interpretation at some length since it is clear that, for the group to which the book is addressed, the knowledge that comes to them in this way is part of the true wisdom. It is not confined to biblical interpretation since, as we have seen, there is only one case of this in Daniel — Jeremiah's seventy-year exile (Dan. 9: 2). At the same time, it is inseparable from a life of intense dedication to the ideal of holiness enshrined in the law. The visionary sage prepares for the revelation by fasting, prayer, and the confession of sin (2: 18; 9: 1-19; 10: 2-3). There is even a suggestion that this kind of activity took place during a service of worship, as seems to have been the case also in early Christianity (cf. Rev. 1: 10). The reception of the revelation called for praise and thanksgiving, as is apparent in the fragments of psalms scattered throughout the book. Here, too, comparison with the Qumran community is useful, specifically with the Hymn Scroll (*Hodayoth*) discovered in the first cave:

> These things I have come to know by thy wisdom,
> For thou hast uncovered my ears to wonderful
>   mysteries. (1: 21)

To sum up: the milieu is quite different from that of the learned Ben Sira and the Wisdom of Solomon yet is, notwithstanding, scribal and sapiential. Speculation and mythic symbolism play a much larger part (even more so in the Enoch cycle which we have not considered), the fusion between learning and piety is much more intense, and the apocalyptic interpretation of history has become the touchstone of faith. The law is never identified with wisdom, though its strict interpretation and observance, sharpened by the conviction of living in the last age, was basic to everything else.

Wisdom in transition: some later developments

While convenient and necessary, our practice of assigning texts to such distinct categories as Apocrypha, Pseudepigrapha, Classical Judaism, etc., may lead us to overlook continuities and similarities which need to be emphasized. 'Wisdom literature' did not, needless to say, come to an end with the closing of the canon, and neither Judaism nor early Christianity was hermetically sealed off from philosophical currents in the Graeco-Roman world. Thus, the practice of collecting the maxims of an exemplary teacher was a common feature of the intellectual life of that time. It is exemplified in the *Enchiridion* of Epictetus (*c.* AD 50–120), a brief manual of theoretical and applied Stoic ethics in the form of sayings. An example would be:

> Demand not that events should happen as you wish; but wish them to happen as they do happen, and you will go on well.

Much of the teaching contained in this work could have been appropriated without alteration by Jewish or Christian teachers. The form was also in common use, e.g., in the Mishnaic tractate *Pirke Aboth* (The Sayings of the Fathers), cited at the end of the previous chapter, and in collections of sayings attributed to Jesus.

Pirke Aboth provides an excellent illustration of the continuity of the sapiential tradition in Judaism. In the first place, its attributions span the period from the second century BC to the time of the compilation of the Mishnah towards the beginning of the second century AD. It takes up many of the themes of the older wisdom as, for example:

All my days I grew up among the sages, and I have found nothing better for myself than silence. (1: 17)

There is also the occasional enigmatic note, as in a saying attributed to the great Hillel:

> If I am not for myself, who is for me?
> And when I am for myself, what am I?
> And if not now, when? (1: 14)

There is, of course, no wisdom without godly fear and the observance of Torah:

> Everyone whose fear of sinning has precedence over his wisdom, his wisdom endures; but everyone whose wisdom has precedence over his fear of sinning, his wisdom does not endure. (3: 11)

In general, these sayings attest to the great importance of the sage in the life of Jewish communities after the destruction of the temple. So, for example, Rabbi Jose ben-Joezer says:

> Let your house be a meeting place for the sages; be dusty with the dust of their feet and thirstily drink up their words. (1: 4)

There is nothing quite comparable to *Aboth* in early Christian literature, though some collections of moral aphorisms were in circulation by the end of the second century AD. One of these, known as *The Sentences of Sextus*, appears to have had the purpose of presenting the Christian life as a noble philosophy which, through wisdom, leads the soul to God. We must recall that in antiquity the philosophical ideal was never purely intellectual, but implied in addition a call to a highly moral and ascetic life. Much of the content of *The Sentences* is not specifically Christian and many of the sayings draw on the aphoristic wisdom of Proverbs and Ecclesiasticus. From the earliest times the needs of Christian communities were met by exchange of correspondence and, in due course, manuals of ecclesiastical discipline comparable in some respects to the Qumran community rules discussed earlier. The first of these known to us, the *Didache* or *Teaching of the Twelve Apostles* from the late first or early second century, contains a first section (chapters

1-6) which is probably Jewish in origin and which stands in direct line of continuity with the older wisdom. The teacher, for example, addresses the neophite as 'son', presents his lesson in the well-established form of the Two Ways, and emphasizes strict control of the passions. Both of these works will illustrate the fact that, in general, the content of early Christian ethics had little to distinguish it from traditional and contemporary Jewish moral teaching.

Collections of sayings attributed to Jesus as wise teacher were made by Gnostic Christians several centuries after his lifetime. One of these, known as the Gospel of Thomas, was discovered at Nag Hammadi in Egypt in 1945. Introduced as 'secret sayings of Jesus', it contains one hundred and fourteen sayings, proverbs, and parables several of which have parallels in the canonical gospels and some few of which, previously unknown, may go back to Jesus himself. For the most part, they present him as dispensing esoteric wisdom to a circle of initiates:

> Jesus said, 'He who will drink from my mouth will become like me. I too will become he, and the secrets will be revealed to him.'

Among the canonical gospels, Matthew is especially interested in presenting Jesus as wise teacher and, to this end, has gathered his sayings into five discourses, doubtless modelled on the five books of Moses. The first of these, the Sermon on the Mount (5-7), concludes with the familiar contrast between the wise person and the fool (7: 24-7), while the parable discourse concludes with what looks like the evangelist's signature:

> Therefore every scribe who has been trained for the kingdom of heaven is like a householder who brings out of his treasure what is new and what is old. (13: 52)

While there is more to the first gospel than that, it does seem to indicate the intention of placing the teaching of Jesus within the continuing tradition of Israelite wisdom.

While the pre-existence of Torah is often a subject of commentary in the midrash, speculation about wisdom similar to what we have seen in Proverbs, Ecclesiasticus, and the Wisdom of Solomon was, for the most part, confined to the mystical tradition. This tradition, which was particularly concerned with speculations based on the biblical creation narrative and Ezekiel's description of the chariot throne, came to mature expression in the medieval *Book of Splendour* (the *Zohar*) and other classics. We noted earlier that the personification of wisdom as co-agent with God in creation was developed in different ways by Jewish intellectual circles in Alexandria, and especially by Philo who lived there during the first half of the first century AD. His description of the Logos (word) or Sophia (wisdom) as an emanation from God bridging the gap between the Creator and the creature was taken over by the Christian school established in the same city. In due course, it provided Origen, the great representative of that school in the third century, with categories in which to express the relationship of Christ to the Father.

Recent study of the New Testament has shown that this line of thought, based on wisdom speculation, emerged even earlier in the history of Christianity. It can be detected in fragments of hymns embedded in the letters (e.g. Col. 1: 15-20) and it seems to have given rise to polemic in the Corinthian church as early as the fifth decade of the first century (1 Cor. 1-2). In the Sayings Source known to modern scholarship as Q (for the German *Quelle*, meaning source), presumed to have been drawn on by Matthew and Luke, Jesus is represented not only as wise teacher but as personified Wisdom (e.g. Mt. 11: 16-19, 25-30; 12: 42; 23: 34-6 and parallels in Luke). Taking everything into account, there can be no doubt that the wisdom of Israel, especially in its later developments traced out in the present chapter, provided a major impetus to the formation of Christian ethics and theology. At this point, however, we have moved beyond the scope of the present volume.

SELECT BIBLIOGRAPHY

Wisdom and Law in General

A. Alt, 'The Origins of Israelite Law', *Essays on Old Testament History and Religion* (Oxford 1966), 79–132

S. H. Blank, 'Wisdom', *The Interpreter's Dictionary of the Bible* IV (Nashville and New York 1962), 852–61

H. J. Boecker, *Law and the Administration of Justice in the Old Testament and Ancient East* (Minneapolis, 1980)

R. E. Clements, 'Interpreting the Pentateuch' and 'Interpreting the Wisdom Literature', *A Century of Old Testament Study* (London 1976), 7–30, 99–117

J. L. Crenshaw, 'Wisdom in the Old Testament', *The Interpreter's Dictionary of the Bible. Supplementary Volume* (Nashville and New York 1976), 952–6

id., *Old Testament Wisdom. An Introduction*. (Atlanta 1981; London 1982)

S. Greengus, 'Laws in the Old Testament', *The Interpreter's Dictionary of the Bible. Supplementary Volume*, 532–7

W. J. Harrelson, 'Law in the Old Testament', *The Interpreter's Dictionary of the Bible* III (Nashville and New York 1962), 77–89

D. R. Hillers, *Covenant. The History of a Biblical Idea* (Baltimore 1969)

G. von Rad, *Wisdom in Israel* (London 1972)

R. B. Y. Scott, *The Way of Wisdom in the Old Testament* (New York 1971)

J. A. Soggin, *Introduction to the Old Testament* (London 1976; rev. ed. 1980)

R. N. Whybray, *The Intellectual Tradition in the Old Testament* (Berlin and New York 1974)

Special Topics and Commentaries

B. S. Childs, *Exodus. A Commentary* (London 1974), especially 337–511 covering the Sinai narrative and the laws

R. J. Coggins, *The First and Second Books of the Chronicles* and *The Books of Ezra and Nehemiah* (Cambridge 1976)

R. Gordis, *Koheleth. The Man and His World* (New York 1951)

M. Hengel, *Judaism and Hellenism* (London 1974), 115–53. The historical background of Ecclesiastes and Ecclesiasticus

W. G. Lambert, *Babylonian Wisdom Literature* (Oxford 1960)

W. McKane, *Prophets and Wise Men* (London 1965)

id., *Proverbs* (London 1970)

A. D. H. Mayes, *Deuteronomy* (New Century Bible. London, 1979)

M. Noth, *Exodus. A Commentary* (London 1962)

id., *A History of Pentateuchal Traditions* (Englewood Cliffs 1972)

M. Pope, *Job* (Garden City 1973)

D. S. Russell, *The Method and Message of Jewish Apocalyptic* (London 1964)

J. J. Stamm and M. E. Andrew, *The Ten Commandments in Recent Research* (London 1967)

M. Stone, *Scriptures, Sects and Visions. A Profile of Judaism from Ezra to the Jewish Revolts* (London 1980)

R. N. Whybray, *Wisdom in Proverbs* (London 1965)

R. L. Wilken (ed.), *Aspects of Wisdom in Judaism and Early Christianity* (Notre Dame 1975) Containing essays on the place of wisdom in the Gospel tradition, early Christian hymns, Paul, Philo, Jewish midrash and the Sentences of Sextus

R. J. Williams, 'Wisdom in the Ancient Near East', *Interpreter's Dictionary of the Bible. Supplementary Volume*, 949–52

D. Winston, *The Wisdom of Solomon* (Garden City 1979)

Non-biblical Material

J. B. Pritchard (ed.), *The Ancient Near East. An Anthology of Texts and Pictures* (Princeton 1958), especially 133–72, legal texts, and 234–52, wisdom material

J. B. Pritchard (ed.), *The Ancient Near East, Volume II: A New Anthology of Texts and Pictures* (Princeton 1975), especially 31–86, laws and treaties, and 136–67, sapiential and didactic texts

INDEX OF PASSAGES CITED

GENERAL INDEX